THE SHAMAN & THE

THE SHAMAN

&

THE STORYTELLER

Michael Berman

Foreword by Jonathan Horwitz

Superscript
The imprint of Cyhoeddwyr y Superscript Ltd,
404 Robin Square
Newtown. SY16 1HP

First published by Superscript, 2005

Front cover by David McClements: www . dmcclements.co.uk

Design by Emma Jane Connolly

ISBN 0954291379

Printed and bound by Antony Rowe, Eastbourne

CONTENTS

Acknowledgements

I would like to thank all the librarians in Swiss Cottage Library for putting up so patiently with me and my pacemaker, and for helping to obtain all the books I needed for my research. Thank you too, David, for your artwork - the time you set aside for it was very much appreciated, especially in view of your other commitments. A special thank you to Leo Rutherford for starting me off on this journey and to Jonathan Horwitz for helping me to find the way forward from there. Thank you Julienne Ford for believing in this project and doing such a professional job of producing the book, and thank you Ketevan for putting up with my single-mindedness. Last but not least, a big thank you to my mum - for without her none of this would ever have been possible.

FOREWORD

During the Inquisition and the years that followed, many people all over Europe who carried the knowledge of shamanism were literally put to the torch. But in recent years shamanism has been experiencing a revival in the modern western world. While academics and religious leaders have been discussing the reasons for this, many people have been quietly getting on with learning the principles and practice of shamanism. Most of the interest in shamanism has been in the shaman's healing ways, the ways of contacting the power of the Universe and the animate world around us. The shaman knows that all that exists is alive, pulsating with energy which is willing to be tapped, bringing power, knowledge, healing, and wisdom to those who need and can use it. In this way the shaman builds a brige between the physical world and the unseen Universe surrounding us.

Because the ability to do shamanic work is a natural ability, many people feel drawn to it. Not only is it empowering, but many feel it gives a sense of purpose, and, at the same time, a feeling of belonging and connection. But what many fail to realize is that, traditionally, the shaman was also the carrier of history and of the knowledge of The People. This history was expressed in the rituals and ceremonies, but especially in the stories which were handed down from generation to generation. For some reason, this aspect of shamanism has been greatly, and sadly, overlooked. Until now.

Michael Berman has been a student of shamanism for many years. In the first part of *The Shaman and the Storyteller*, he gives a thorough introduction to the study, history, and practice of shamanism. And well he knows. His own practice of shamanism goes back some fifteen years, and he has clearly learned his lessons well, showing a seriousness, clarity of intent, and absence of self-importance which often otherwise seem missing in this brave new world we live in.

In the second part of the book he weaves in the art and magic of the storyteller, showing clearly the unity of the shaman and the storyteller, and indeed how many of our best loved stories, including some from the Bible, clearly have their roots in the times when our own ancestors were animists, practising shamanism. Indeed, he shows clearly the healing power of the story, something the shaman has never been blind to, by putting the patient into the myth, connecting her to the very power which created the Universe.

My own hope is that those who practise shamanism and read this book will see the opportunity for deepening their practice through the telling of their experiences in ways which can benefit the rest of the community. I also hope that storytellers who read this will be inspired to learn to walk the path of the shaman.

The wisdom offered us from the Power of the Universe is desperately needed at this time. Our own history is now being told by the mass media. We deserve more than this, as do our children, and our children's children. Our history and our stories need to be told by visionaries, wise women and men who can see beneath the surface, beyond the seas, and over the mountains, bringing home the truths of our lives from beyond the Moon or the dandelion growing by the bus-stop.

May you be inspired.

Jonathan Horwitz
Scandinavian Center for Shamanic Studies
Copenhagen, Denmark.

A Definition and a Brief History of Shamanism

The suggestion that the shaman is 'possessed' is frequently found in definitions. It will be shown, by providing examples to support the case, that such a suggestion is unhelpful as in fact he is very much in control of the process he initiates. Indeed, if he was not in control of the process, he would surely be unable to do his job effectively and would thus not be accepted as a shaman by the community in which he operates.

As Lewis points out, the Tungus, for example, distinguish between a person who is possessed (involuntarily) by a spirit, and a spirit possessed (voluntarily) by a person (Lewis, I.M., 2003). In the case of those who persist in the shamanistic calling, the uncontrolled, unsolicited, initial possession seizure leads to a state where possession can be controlled and can be turned off at will. Paul Radin suggests that 'the primary function of the medicine man ... was to act as an intermediator. Just as his primary task was to develop a type of approach to the supernatural that would appeal to the layman and furnish him with explanations for success or failure that would be acceptable, the shaman's role as intermediary had to be accepted and respected, and his ministrations had to become sufficiently remunerative to give him both economic security and a measure of independence' (Radin, P., 1957, p.172). None of this would have been remotely possible if he had not been very much in control of what he did.

This is what Michael Harner has to say on the subject: '... in all these activities [journeying to "nonordinary reality"], the shaman usually remains conscious and in control of his or her own faculties and will, and typically suffers no amnesia upon returning to ordinary reality. ... the shaman can remember later what took place in the spirit world, whereas the medium generally comes out of the altered state without substantial memory of the events that transpired during the time of possession' (Harner in Doore, G. (Ed.), 1988, p.8). Harner reinforces the point by adding that 'shamans are typically very well grounded in this ordinary reality – so grounded that they can in fact move over into that other dimension with discipline and focus, which is the only way to be effective in helping others' (*Ibid.* p.12). He also points out in *The Way of the Shaman* that 'Even when shamans dance their guardian animal spirits', this is 'not the uncontrollable possession of the Carribean Vodun cults, but rather a reaffirmation by the shaman of his oneness with his animal companion'. As Eliade notes, this is 'less a possession than a magical transformation of the shaman into that animal' (Harner, M., 1990 Third Edition, pp.62-63).

In Shamanism, rapture can be seen as one method of enhancing life's powerfulness. 'Whether or not this inspiration is ascribed to demonic possession it is in any case an affair of decreasing one's own, and increasing a foreign, numinous and demonic life; the ancient Israelite judges, for example, led their people to victory because the spirit of Jahveh had come upon them. This exaltation, this fullness of God, confers mighty power' (Van Der Leeuw, G., 1938, p.487). Viewed in this light, 'possession' can be seen as something positive and worth striving for, without the usual negative connotations associated with the word.

As Michael Harner points out, 'In a dream, you may not be able to extricate yourself voluntarily from an unwanted experience or nightmare. In contrast, one wills himself into the SSC [Shamanic State of Consciousness] and, since it is a conscious waking state, is able at any time to will himself out of it, back into the [Ordinary State of Consciousness] OSC' (Harner, M., 1990, p.xxii). However, it has to be conceded that when powerful hallucinogenic drugs are taken by the shaman, it may not be so easy for him to will himself out of it at any time. Nevertheless, it is clear that the shaman is very much in control of the process and the suggestion that he/she is 'possessed' creates a false impression of what actually takes place.

There is a danger of what Michael Harner calls 'cognicentricism' – interpreting alternative states from the limited perspective and experience of our own state – and this is undoubtedly what has happened in the past. 'Western psychiatry has a long history of viewing mystics as madmen, saints as psychotics, and sages as schizophrenics' (Walsh, R. N.,1990, p.75). 'Religious experiences and states of consciousness have been viewed all too often as pathological because of cultural bias, lack of psychological expertise, psychoanalytic emphasis on pathology, and ignorance of the potential range and value of certain altered states' (*Ibid.* p.76). 'The shaman has control over the trance, entering and leaving it at will. This is quite different from the classic dissociative disorders, which appear to overtake and control their victims. ... In the clinical dissociative disorders, the dissociation functions as a defence mechanism by reducing and distorting consciousness in order to avoid the awareness of psychological pain and conflict. [However,] the shamanic journey seems to do almost the opposite' (Walsh, R. N., 1990, pp. 81-82).

The main differences between the shaman and the schizophrenic, to whom he has been wrongly compared, are neatly summarized by Vitebsky: 'Where the shaman's concentration is increased, that of the schizophrenic is scattered; where the shaman retains a far-reaching control of his or her own state of mind, schizophrenia entails a loss of this control; and where the shaman's experience is always brought back to society and shared for society's benefit, the schizophrenic is trapped inside a private experience, almost to the point of autism' (Vitebsky, P., 2001, p.138).

Rowena Pattee explains very clearly why the belief that the shaman is possessed is a misconception, and hopefully the following quote will settle this issue once and for all: 'Certain forms of channelling and of possession by spirits are

3

characterized by total amnesia of the experience, whereas other forms of both immobile practices (prayer and meditation) and frenzied practices (shamanic drumming, chanting, dancing) of ecstasy are fully conscious. ... The state of amnesia I regard as a state of possession wherein the will of the participant is set aside, whether in religions or shamanism'(in Doore, G. (Ed.), 1988, p.20). 'The willingly induced state of the inspired I take to be more the state of both the shaman and religious mystics whom Eliade calls prophets, whereas the involuntary state of possession is more like a psychotic state. Although both the shaman and religious mystics may have been possessed during their "call," their empowerment lies in the fact that they have overcome the involuntary, helpless, victimized state of spirit-possession and are cured. The shaman seeks to cure possession, not be possessed' (*Ibid.* p.22).

The fact of the matter is that, based on innumerable accounts recorded by anthropologists and also based on accounts of personal experiences, the master shaman is at all times in control of the process. 'The shaman moves back and forth between the two realities deliberately and with serious intention. Whichever the reality, the shaman thinks and acts in the ways appropriate to it, and has as his objective the mastery of both his nonordinary activities and his ordinary activities. Only he who successfully masters his actions in both realms is a master shaman' (Harner, M., 1990, pp.46-47). ... 'the shaman recognizes the separateness of the SSC reality from that of the OSC, and does not confuse the two. He knows when he is one or the other, and enters each by choice' (*Ibid.* p.53). The SSC normally permits full recall later of the experience when the shaman has returned to the OSC, unlike the characteristic trance of the Western spirit medium or of the participant in Caribbean or Javanese spirit possession dances' (*Ibid.* p.50). Once again it can be seen that the term 'possession' is inappropriate for describing the typical shamanic state. Even when shamans dance their guardian animal spirits, this is 'not the uncontrollable possession of the Carribean Vodun cults', but rather a reaffirmation by the shaman of his oneness with his animal companion. As Eliade, quoted by Harner, notes, this is 'less a possession than a magical transformation of the shaman into that animal' (*Ibid*. pp.62-63).

Jung, however, maintained that conscious man does not possess the unconscious, rather he is possessed by it, so in that sense we can all be said to be possessed!

It is also falsely supposed by some writers that shamans are, and/or were, exclusively male. As Gustav Rank points out, 'A large number of Russian scholars build their theory about female shamans and their priority in time to male shamans on such supposed survivals [of earlier stages of development]. The theoretical background to this assumption is made up of the evolutionist conception of history according to which the whole of mankind has gone through a matriarchal phase in which the woman was not only the head of the family but also a seer and priest' (in Edsman, C.M. (Ed.), 1967, pp.16-17). However, concrete evidence to indicate that the original shamans were in fact women has not been produced to date. On the other hand, there is plenty of evidence to indicate that women have played an important part in the history of shamanism, as the following quotes clearly show:

'The priestess of the Bahaus of Borneo brings the soul of a sick person back along the "soul road", fastened to a cord after she has enticed it to her; then she blows the soul back into the body through the skull' (Nieuwenhuis, *Wurzeln*, 43; *cf*. his *Quer durch Borneo*, I, 103, quoted in Van Der Leeuw, 1938, p.296).

'The Korean *son-mudang*, the Ainu *tsusu*, the Ryukyu *yuta*, all testify to a wide area where once a feminine shamanism of a northern, Siberian type was dominant, where sacral power was believed to reside more easily and properly in women, and where in consequence women were recognized to be the natural intermediaries between the two worlds' (Blacker, C. ,1999, p.28).

'The oldest shamanic figure of which we have any record is the Shinto miko. This powerful sacral woman – the term "female shaman" conveys only feebly the probable majesty of her presence – served in shrines throughout the land in the late prehistoric period as the mouthpiece for numina of certain kinds' (Blacker, C., 1999, p.104).

'Magic power, similar to that inhering in the kami, was in the Ryukyu [islands] controlled and invoked only by women. A man who required such power for the exercise of his office, and secular offices were usually held by men, was entirely dependent on a woman relative for its acquisition' (Blacker, C., 1999, p.113).

The following quote appears to demean women, but bear in mind that it comes from a book published in 1923: 'Women sometimes are considered superior enough to attain the coveted position [of shaman]. In *Die Medizin der Naturvolker*, Doctor Bartels asserts that this is the case among the Ashanti, among the people of Loango, 'in Libuku, in Zululand, in Borneo, in Australia, in Siberia, and among some of our Indian tribes' (Maddox, J. L., 2003, p.72).

'In Siberia', writes Sieroshevski, 'The shamanesses have greater power than the shamans; in general, the feminine element plays a very prominent role in sorcery among the Yakuts. In the Kolmyck district the shamans for want of any special dress put on the dress of women. They wear their hair long and comb and braid it as women do' (Maddox, J. L., 2003, p.88).

'In Korea, the female idea of the shamanate prevails to such an extent that the men who take up the profession wear female clothing while performing their duties, and the whole shaman class is spoken of as feminine' (Maddox, J.L., 2003, p.88).

6

'In Korea, the *Mugam,* usually a woman, is called in to fulfil the role of psychopomp when someone dies. A séance or *kut* is then held at the family's expense. In trance, the *mugam* summons the Death Messenger who is offered various bribes to ensure generous treatment for the deceased. The *mugam* will also communicate with the lingering spirit of the deceased, persuading him to leave his old abode and to accept his new home and status, explaining the arrangements made with the Death Messenger for his reception. The climax of the ceremonies is when a strip of white silken cloth is stretched between two of the mourners to serve as a bridge. The *mugam* splits it with a knife and pushes her own body along it, so dividing it into two narrower strips. As she does so she pushes in front of her various belongings of the dead, often including his photograph. When she reaches the further end it is believed the spirit has now been safely conducted to its new abode. The ritual ends with the destruction of the cloth bridge' (Rutherford, W., 1986, p.78).

Vitebsky makes the point that, generally speaking, female shamans are 'more prominent in agrarian, crop-growing societies, as is the case in South and Southeast Asia' (Vitebsky, P., 2001, p.33). He also observes that '[among] the Sora, an aboriginal jungle tribe in Orissa, India … the "great" shamans, who are mostly women, conduct funerals while the "lesser" shamans, mostly men, perform divinations and cures' *(Ibid* p.40).

There is even a tradition among certain tribal groups that the first shamans were in fact female. 'A Buryat story of the origins of shamanism tells how the first shaman sent to humans by the gods was an eagle – the bird could not make himself understood but he had sexual intercourse with a woman to whom shamanic abilities were thereby transferred' (Stone, A., 2003, p.54).

Many other quotes describing women shamans could have been included but for reasons of space this will have to suffice. Hopefully there can now be no doubt that women have played a significant role in the history of shamanism, and indeed they continue to do so, especially in neo-shamanism.

There is also plenty of evidence to show that women have had a full part to play in the history of healing:

> In Egypt, peculiar medical skill was assigned to Isis, the wife and sister of Osiris. Tradition had it that she gave unequivocal proof of her power by restoring Horus, her son, to life. She was believed to have discovered several remedies, and the material medica of the time of Galen contained drugs that were named in her honor. ... Among the Greeks, Hygeia, daughter of Aesculapius, god of medicine, was worshipped in the temples of Argos as the goddess of both physical and mental health. ... This information, although derived from fabled story, serves the important purpose of preserving in allegoric form facts from which the inference is to be drawn that in remote antiquity women engaged in the practice of medicine. (Maddox, J. L., 2003, p.75).

> ... cases are on record in all stages of the history of the world in which, through force of circumstances, or, more often, through force of character, women have frequently acquired surgical skill, and often pursued successfully the divine art of healing. (*Ibid*, pp.76-77).

Another misconception about women in shamanism is the theory, put forward by Lewis, that symptoms of malevolent spirit possession are an unconscious attempt by women to protest against neglect and oppression in a society largely dominated by men (*op.cit*). Evidence to disprove the theory can be found in Blacker's book: '[Although] in all districts of Japan where cases of malignant possession occur, the large majority of patients are always women ... none of the patients ... derive any satisfaction from becoming the unwanted centre of attention among usually neglectful men. Nor are the rewards demanded by the spirit comparable with the sewing machines or soap demanded by the Somali women [cited by Lewis]' (Blacker, 1999, pp.312-313). Although instances such as those cited by Lewis clearly occur, it would be wrong to generalize and infer from them that this is always the case.

Now let us take a look at some of the definitions of shamanism put forward by various experts in the field. To start off with, some information on the etymology of the word:

> The late Professor Vilmos Dioszegi, writing in the fifteenth edition of *Encyclopedia Britannica*, finds its derivation in the Tungoso-Manchurian word *saman*, formed from the verb *sa-*. This implies a relationship with the Indo-European root yielding the French *savoir* and the Spanish *saber*, both meaning 'to know'. In this way the shaman becomes 'he who knows', giving the word an etymological relationship to such familiar words as 'witch' and 'wizard', both from Indo-European root meaning 'to see' or 'to know', and present in the forms of the French *voir*, the Latin *videre*, to see, and the German *wissen*, 'to know'. (Rutherford, W., 1986, p.15).

In 1944 Swiss anthropologist Alfred Metraux defined the shaman as 'any individual who maintains by profession and in the interests of the community an intermittent commerce with spirits, or who is possessed by them' (quoted in Narby, J., & Huxley, F., 2001, p.4). 'While Metraux's definition is appealing in its simplicity and even-handedness, it is perhaps ultimately too broad, as it also fits African and Haitian possession cults. So we would add to Metraux's definition: Shamanism involves a kind of theatre in which the shaman performs and the audience remains an audience' (*Ibid.* p.78). The words 'by profession' remain a problem, however, as shamans, especially in small communities, often had other full-time occupations as well.

In the words of Eliade, 'The shaman specializes in a trance during which his soul is believed to leave his body and ascend to the sky or descend to the underworld' (Eliade, 1964, p.5). This definition, however, would appear to be somewhat incomplete as the shaman undertakes other journeys too. Eliade then goes on to add the point that 'the shaman controls his "spirits," in the sense that he, a human being, is able to communicate with the dead, "demons," and "nature spirits," without thereby becoming their instrument' (*Ibid.* p.6). There is no sense here of the shaman being 'possessed' so it can be regarded as a useful addition.

Harner basically agrees with Eliade. He defines a shaman as 'a man or woman who enters an altered state of consciousness – at will – to contact and utilize an ordinarily hidden reality in order to acquire knowledge, power, and to help other persons. The shaman has at least one, and usually more, "spirits" in his personal service. As Mircea Eliade observes, the shaman is distinguished from other kinds of magicians and medicine men by his use of a state of consciousness which Eliade, following Western mystical tradition, calls "ecstasy"' (Harner, M., 1990 Third Edition, p.20).

Eliade finds that the shaman is distinguished from the medicine-man, the magician and the sorcerer 'by a magico-religious technique which is in a way exclusive to him and which may be called: the ecstatic's trip to Heaven, to the Lower World, or to the depths of the ocean' (Eliade, M., 1950). Hultkrantz, however, believes 'that this definition is too limited; it is at least as characteristic for the shaman to operate without any extra-corporeal journey to the other world, provided he is in an ecstatic state' (Edsman, C.M. (ed.), 1967, p.32). In view of the variety of techniques employed by shamans, my inclination is to agree with him.

Lewis 'emphasises the coincident importance of spirit possession and [also] rejects the shaman's 'celestial voyage', as the determining feature insisted on by Eliade and his successors' (Lewis, I.M., 2003 Third Edition, p.xviii). He paraphrases Eliade's definition, but only so as to criticize it: 'According to Mircea Eliade, the diagnostic features of shamanism in the classical Arctic sense are quite specific. The shaman is an inspired priest who, in ecstatic trance, ascends to the heavens on 'trips'. However, you can be sure that Eliade never used the word 'trip'. Lewis then goes on to add, 'In the course of these journeys he persuades or even fights with the gods in order to secure benefits for his fellow men. Here, in the opinion of Eliade, spirit possession is not an essential characteristic and is not always present' (*Ibid*, p.43). Nowhere in Eliade's writings will you find the suggestion the shaman 'fights' with the gods; once again Lewis's intention is clearly to put Eliade down.

Lewis then goes on to point out that 'shamanism and spirit possession regularly occur together and this is true particularly in the Arctic *locus classicus* of shamanism. Thus, amonst the Eskimos and the East Siberian Chukchee, shamans are possessed by spirits. More significantly still, this is also true of the Arctic Tungus from whose language the word shaman derives, and whom, therefore we may take to epitomize the phenomena under discussion' (*Ibid*. pp.44-45). Lewis seems to fail to appreciate that the shaman calls and then directs the spirits he works with to attend to his concerns and has much more control over the process or else he would surely be ineffective in his efforts to help the clients who turn to him. The next point that Lewis makes is that 'The Tungus distinguish between a person possessed (involuntarily) by a spirit, and a spirit possessed (voluntarily) by a person … In the case of those who persist in the shamanistic calling, the uncontrolled, unsolicited, initial possession seizure leads to a state where possession can be controlled and can be turned off at will in shamanistic séances' (*Ibid*. p.48). Since Lewis indeed recognizes this ability that shamans have, then surely he should include it in his definition!

According to Blacker, 'The shaman is, first, a person who receives a supernatural gift from the spirit world. ... the ability to put himself at will into altered states of consciousness in which he can communicate directly with spiritual beings. ... He is given indispensable help in this task, first by a retinue of assistant spirits and secondly by a panoply of magic clothes' (Blacker, C., 1999, pp.24-25). 'He must be capable of offering his body as a vessel for possession by spirits' (*Ibid.* p.26). However, nearly all her research is based on her trips to Japan and the 'magic clothes' are not necessarily always a common feature. 'Louise Backman and Ake Hultkrantz are of the opinion that, with the Lapps, special apparel was not regarded as at all necessary. They suggest that items labelled as Noaidic costume in the museums of Oslo and Stockholm are likely to belong to a late phase when the calling was in decay and the Noaidit were trying to impart respectability to it by emulating the vestments of the clergy' (Rutherford, W., 1986, p.44). Moreover, as has already been pointed out, it can be argued that the shaman is very much in control of the process rather than being merely a 'vessel for possession,' as Blacker suggests.

In the view of Radin, 'The shaman was first and foremost a physician and a curer. His neurotic-epileptoid constitution came to his aid here, for was he not, in a sense, periodically ill? He differed from the generality of mankind, however, not only because he possessed such a special and diseased mentality but because he was at the same time endowed with the power to cure himself' (Radin, P., 1957, pp.134-135). He then goes on to define the shaman in terms of the role he performs: 'The initial and primary task of the shaman-priest is to emphasize and magnify the obstacles that stand between man and his natural and realistic adjustment to the outside world. It is through the excellence and effectiveness of the "technique of obstacles" that he made his living and retained his hold upon the imagination of the people. Nor does this necessarily imply that he was an impostor, a dupe, or an individual with only mercenary motives' (*Ibid.* p.145).

As for Sandra Ingermann's definition, she would also appear to regard the shaman as primarily a healer: 'A shamanic practitioner journeys to the spiritual realms on the client's behalf to gather information on the appropriate method of healing in a particular case' (Ingermann, S., 1993, p.23). Ake Hultkrantz defines a shaman 'as an inspired visionary who, on behalf of the society he serves, and with the assistance of his guardian spirits, enters into a deep trance in which his dreaming ego establishes relations with spiritual powers' (in Doore, G. (Ed.), 1988, pp.34-35). This definition, like Ingermann's, is likely to appeal to those who place an emphasis on the therapeutic aspect of the shaman's work. It would also prove to be acceptable to the neo-shamanists.

Richard Noll – an American clinical psychologist - defines shamanism as 'an ecstatic healing tradition which at its core is concerned with the techniques for inducing, maintaining, and interpreting the vivid experiences of enhanced mental imagery that occur in the deliberately induced altered states of consciousness in the shaman' (Narby, J., & Huxley, F., 2001, p.249). However, the suggestion that it involves 'inducing' an experience from something already induced seems to me a somewhat clumsy use of words and neo-shamans such as Michael Harner or Jonathan Horwitz would do no 'interpreting' of the experience as that would disempower the client.

Although Roger Walsh, like many others, approves of Harner's definition, he concludes by encapsulating just why the choice of an appropriate definition is such a tricky business, and just why no two people seem to be able to agree on what that definition should be: 'In all Tungus languages this term (saman) refers to persons of both sexes who have mastered spirits, who at their will can introduce these spirits into themselves and use their power over the spirits in their own interests, particularly helping other people, who suffer from the spirits (Shirokogoroff, S.,1935, p.269). Should these two additional elements, [in Harner's definition] contacting a hidden reality and interaction with spirits, be included as essential elements of a definition of shamanism? ... Certainly these elements describe what shamans experience and believe they are doing ... [but] the interpretation of the nature of these phenomena depends on one's own philosophical leanings or world view' (Walsh, R. N., 1990, p.11).

Hultkrantz has proposed that there are in fact three different types of shamanism: genuine **ecstatic** shamanism, **imitative** shamanism and **demonstrative** shamanism. In the case of the **imitative** form, the shaman enacts a kind of ritual pantomime or seance, and in the **demonstrative** form the shaman proves his success in curing the sick by, for example, holding up for all to see the disease object that he has extracted from the patient (Hultkrantz, 1979, p.91).

Although **imitative** and **demonstrative** shamanism may be little more than theatrical performances, this does not invalidate them as they can be just as effective in practice as **ecstatic** shamanism, and what is of primary importance is surely whether the process works or not. There is, of course, the possibility that the different types of shamanism described by Hultkrantz could also be used in tandem with each other. Neo-shamanism can, in fact, take the form of any of the three types of shamanism described above, or an amalgam of all three.

As for the origin of shamanism, 'nothing justifies the supposition that during the hundreds of thousands of years that preceded the earliest Stone Age, humanity did not have a religious life as intense and as various as in the succeeding periods' (Eliade, M., 1989, p.5).

It was believed until recently that shamanism dated back to Paleolithic times.

Europe has the oldest evidence – animal skulls and bones believed to be shamanic ritual offerings found at sites inhabited between 50,000 and 30,000 B.C. The soundest evidence suggestive of shamanic practices came with the discovery of petroglyphs on the walls of prehistoric caves such as the Lascaux in France and the Altamira in Spain. Shamanic beings depicted in the Lascaux caves were engraved and painted in about 15,000 B.C. Here we find the figure of a "bird-headed man," indicative of flight and a capacity for the ecstatic journey, profiles of deer, horses, cows, and bulls thought to be spirit helpers; and a unicorn figure sometimes interpreted as a "shaman in a skin" driving horses. In 1994 a still older cave was unearthed in France. The Chauvet cave – replete with splendid drawings of horses, bison, rhinoceroses, lions, and an owl – is thought to date back more than 32,000 years. These figures, too, suggest the presence of shamanic activity. (Gagan, J. M., 1998, p.19)

The accuracy of the assumptions presented above, however, is now in doubt. As Stone points out,

the case for these composite cave figures being shamans rests on slender evidence that is not really evidence at all – only interpretation. ... Whatever the figures were intended to represent – and while they might well have been intended to represent shamans it is equally possible that they could have been intended as humour, for instance – such interpretations are not evidence for Palaeolithic European shamanism (Stone, A., 2003, pp. 131-132)

Stone goes on to add that,

the only compelling evidence for continuity of shamanic tradition from ancient times to the present is that from Siberia examined by Hoppal and Devlet. The evidence consists of a number of pictures of shamans with costumes, drums and drumsticks, some in scenes that appear to

15

represent shamanic performance, and at least one showing what seems to be a flying shaman complete with drum and drumstick. None are earlier than about 2000 BC. (*Ibid.* p.140)

So in fact we have no proof at all for the claims made based on the cave figures found in France and Spain.

However, what we can be reasonably sure of is that 'the passing on of shamanic traditions, unlike that of others, did not occur solely through the transference of information from generation to generation or from groups of people living close together. Other possibilities exist. Perhaps the migration of prehistoric civilizations from place to place contributed to the universality of core shamanic practices. Or perhaps an evolution of human consciousness galvanized by common needs, ideologies, mythologies, or religious intents evoked a collective expression' (Gagan, J., 1998, pp.20-21). Trubshaw, however, points out that 'in recent decades archaeologists have largely rejected the idea that the introduction of new cultural ideas (which includes language) necessarily implies a large-scale movement of populations' (Trubshaw, B., 2003, p.37). He goes on to propose that 'there is a shared tradition of myths, rituals, and thinking about the nature of the universe and society. This may be attributable to a combination of one or more processes of sharing, such as common genetic origin, diffusion, and overlapping circles of influence' (*Ibid.* p.37). Walsh takes the proposition one stage further by suggesting that 'shamanism and its widespread distribution may [in fact] reflect an innate human tendency to enter certain pleasurable and valuable states of consciousness. Once discovered, rituals and beliefs that support the induction and expression of these states also arise and shamanism then emerges' (Walsh, R. N., 1990, p.14).

As Michael Harner points out, 'One of the most remarkable things about shamanic assumptions and methods is that they are very similar in widely separated and remote

16

parts of the planet, including such regions as aboriginal Australia, native North and South America, Siberia and Central Asia, eastern and northernmost Europe, and southern Africa. Even in the historical literature from the Classical Mediterranean, or from medieval and Renaissance western Europe, one finds evidence that the same basic shamanic knowledge once existed there until it was largely eradicated by the Inquisition' (Harner, M., 1990 Third Edition, p.41). To this list can be added both Japan and Korea in the Far East, evidence for which can be found in Carmen Blacker's fascinating book (Blacker,C.,1999). Harner than goes on to ask why shamanic knowledge is so basically consistent in different parts of the primitive world, and the answer he comes up with is, quite simply, **because it works**.

Unfortunately, however, it has to be conceded that the world view that has found expression through shamanism in the past is fast disappearing, and it is probably only through neo-shamanism that the traditional practices will continue in some form.

> The vision of another plane utterly different from our own, ambivalent, perilous and beyond our control, has faded. Instead the universe has become one-dimensional; there is no barrier to be crossed, no mysteriously other kind of being to be met and placated. ... When the view of the other world fades, and its inhabitants dwindle to the predictable regularities called the laws of nature, the shaman and his powers are no longer needed. (Blacker, C., 1999, p.315).

A Religion, a Way of Life or a Methodology?

The question of whether shamanism is a religion or a way of life will now be considered:

It would seem that for some people the word religion has negative connotations and they do their best to avoid it at all costs – partly perhaps because it is unfashionable, partly perhaps because it is so difficult to define. Neo-shamanic movements tend to take the view that shamanism is 'opposed to institutionalized religion and political systems and speak of a democratization of shamanism in which every person can be empowered to become their own shaman. They think of shamanism not so much as a religion but as a view of reality and an effective technique' (Vitebsky, P., 2001, p.151).

Sandra Ingermann refers to shamanism as a 'system' and 'a path to accessing spiritual information' (Ingermann, S., 1993, p.4). Michael Harner describes it as a 'methodology', rather than as a religion. He says 'Shamanism represents the most widespread and ancient methodological system of mind-body healing known to humanity' (Harner, M., 1990 Third Edition, p.40). As William James points out, 'the process of remedying inner incompleteness and reducing inner discord is a general psychological process, which may take place with any sort of mental material, and need not necessarily assume the religious form' (James, W., 1982, p.175).

It could be argued that perhaps both Ingermann and Harner are intentionally begging the question and they are not alone in this respect. Another way of avoiding the issue can be found in the following quote taken from an article by Ake Hultkrantz: 'For some people religion is supposed to mean institutionalized religion with a priesthood and a growing class society. In this light, shamanism is of course a pre-religious phenomenon' (Doore, G., (Ed.), 1988, p.36). Even Eliade himself does something similar when he describes it as an 'archaic technique'.

The way in which the respected authorities quoted above skirt the issue of whether shamanism is a religion or not is hardly surprising as any attempt to define the word 'religion' is fraught with difficulty. Some definitions are substantive in that they state what religion is and relate it to an underlying sacred 'substance'. Examples of this type could include Schleiermacher's: 'The feeling of absolute dependence. A sense and taste for the infinite.' Another example is provided by Anthony Wallace: 'a set of rituals, rationalized by myth, which mobilizes supernatural powers for the purpose of achieving or preventing transformations of state in man or nature.' Some definitions are functional and state what religion does and the way it functions in our lives. An example of this type is Malinowski's suggestion that religion 'relieves anxiety and enhances social integration.' Some definitions are too broad and allow things not ordinarily considered to be 'religion' to be included. Alfred North Whitehead's definition provides a good example of this type: 'what the individual does with his own solitariness.' Another example would be what Paul Tillich proposes: 'A person's ultimate concern.' Some definitions, on the other hand, are too narrow and exclude aspects that many people would passionately defend as religious. For example, such definitions might include belief in a personal deity or some supernatural entities. This excludes such non-theistic religions as Buddhism and religious Satanism which have no such belief. Some definitions equate 'religion' with 'Christianity,' and thus define two out of every three humans in the world as non-religious. Finally, some definitions are so ideological that they are of little value to us in a work of this type. Karl Marx, for example, defined religion as 'the sigh of the oppressed creature, the heart of a heartless world, and the soul of soulless conditions. It is the opium of the people.'

In view of the difficulties involved in coming up with an acceptable definition, it might be more helpful if we instead listed what religions tend to consist of. However, let me start by saying what the concept does not necessarily include. Contrary to what many people might expect, '... the idea of a god who is in some way or other personal is not an absolutely necessary element in the structure of religion . ... The names of things subsist before they acquire a "personality"; and the name of God is there even before "God" exists' (Van Der Leeuw, G., 1938, p.147).

Now for what religions do consist of: For example, most religions are organized around certain past events with their own Creation Myths, and these are ordinarily preserved in oral traditions or in sacred writings. Another feature of religions is the way they provide for continual renewal by setting aside special times to celebrate what they hold sacred - festivals and observances that intensify and renew the spiritual memory of their followers. Religions also establish sacred spaces - places of natural beauty, imposing power, or sites that commemorate great religious events of the past. Rites of Passage also tend to play an important part in most religions - birth rites, rites of entry into adulthood, weddings and funerals. Another common feature is the way in which religions involve interaction with Spiritual Beings. – through prayer, offerings and sacrifices, purification and penance, and worship. Sometimes these are regular events, and sometimes they are performed in times of special need. The gods, in turn, are believed to make their presence known to humans in a variety of ways, including prophecy, states of trance, dreams and visions, divination, healings, special signs and miracles, intuition, and mystical experiences. Last but not least, it can be said that most religions provide the opportunity for both Inner Transformation, and Salvation.

Kenneth Meadows points out however, that unlike most religions, shamanism 'is not a belief system at all for it propagates no doctrines' (Meadows, 1991, p.4). And, as he continues,

20

In shamanism you simply **do** it in order to **know** it; knowledge comes through the **doing**. There is no set of beliefs to be accepted before progress can be made; no dogma or creed to be bound up by; no sacred writings to be revered and interpreted, literalized or allegorized; no hierarchy to demand devotion; no vows to be sworn. Only the power source that is within to be awakened and guidelines needed to point the way (*Ibid.* p.5).

However, it can be argued that this is no longer strictly true, as the writings of neo-shamanic practitioners such as Harner are certainly both revered and interpreted by his followers. Moreover, within organisations such as the Foundation for Shamanic Studies there is certainly a hierarchy – with only those who have passed approved courses being officially recognized as practitioners.

Vitebsky suggests that 'Shamanism is not only a religion or a facet of religion, it is a very active and practical one' (Vitebsky, P., 2001, p.156). However, this makes little sense as surely it cannot be 'a religion or a facet of religion': it is either one or the other.

Rennie takes the view that 'since both religion and myth lack predetermined and widely accepted definitions, it is part of the task of scholars of religion to establish their own' (Rennie, 1996, p.184). 'Observable facts seem to concur with Eliade that humanity everywhere throughout history has been classifiable as "religious" in some, possibly unrecognized, way and that contemporary humanity is no different, despite a unique existential situation and an unshakable conviction in the meaning and significance of manifest event. One must wonder whether psychology could have ever coherently constituted itself if some people were allowed to have no psyche, or sociology if some people had no society' (*Ibid.*, p.116). Eliade has also said that religion 'does not necessarily imply belief in God, gods, or ghosts, but refers to the experience of the sacred' (Eliade, M., 1969). And this is surely

21

what is experienced by not only the shaman but also those who witness or participate in his practices. It can consequently be argued that both shamanism and neo-shamanism are indeed religions in the way in which Eliade understood the term. The problem, however, is that this might not be a label that neo-shamanists would necessarily be comfortable with.

Jung once described religions as 'psychotherapeutic systems … We [psychotherapists] are trying to heal the suffering of the human mind, of the human psyche or the human soul, and religion deals with the same problem' (Jung, C.G., 1977, p.162). If you share the belief that this is what religion is, then shamanism can surely be classified under this heading, especially in view of the way it is made use of by healers and therapists. However, religion clearly means different things to different people and not everyone would agree to such a definition.

Paul Radin suggests religion includes 'a belief in spirits outside of man, conceived of as more powerful than man and as controlling all those elements in life upon which he lays most stress' (Radin, P., 1957, p.3). However, some neo-shamanists would argue that 'rather than there actually being other universes, [and spirits outside of man] the beliefs and associated rituals [can] serve to dramatise aspects of the quest within' (Heelas, P., 1996, p.89). They might also be of the opinion that through shamanic practices we can in fact take control of our lives. Consequently, this definition would seem to be unsatisfactory too.

Durkheim defines religion as 'a unified system of beliefs and practices relative to sacred things, that is to say, things set apart and forbidden - beliefs and practices which unite into one single moral community called a Church, all those who adhere to them.' He argues that the really religious beliefs 'are always common to a determined group or 'Church,' which makes a profession of adhering to them and of practicing the rites connected with them.... The individuals which compose it feel themselves united to each other by the simple fact that they have a common faith.' He differentiates between religion and belief in magic by suggesting that the latter 'does not result in binding together those who adhere to it, nor in uniting them into a group leading a common life' (Jones, R.A., 1986, pp. 115-155). There are, however, both solitary witches who celebrate their beliefs by themselves and societies of magicians. Consequently, there would seem to be religions without any churches as well as moral communities of magicians, and for these reasons it has to be concluded that Durkheim's definition is too exclusive.

William James defined religion as '*the feelings, acts, and experiences of individual men in their solitude, so far as they apprehend themselves to stand in relation to whatever they may consider to be the divine.* Since the relation may be either moral, physical, or ritual, it is evident that out of religion in the sense in which we take it, theologies, philosophies, and ecclesiastical organizations may secondarily grow ' (James, W., 1982, p.31). By this definition shamanism would be regarded as a religion. However, it has to be remembered that James 'saw institutions as compromisers of the religious impulse', as Martin E. Marty points out in the Introduction to the Penguin edition of the book. This is probably why the core definition in italics makes no mention of the communal places of worship in which most religions are practised, or the organizations that regulate and monitor such practice. As Jean Houston notes, referring specifically to shamanism, 'one can have one's spiritual experience and revelation direct and unmediated by structures ordained by church and doctrine. This appeals immensely to those who seek autonomy in the spiritual journey' (Houston, J., 1987, p.vii). This aspect of shamanism would presumably have appealed to James too. However, for those who consider institution and doctrine to be an integral part of religious life, the definition put forward by James above would appear to be somewhat incomplete and unsatisfactory.

William James also wrote that 'prayer is religion in act; that is, prayer is real religion. It is prayer that distinguishes the religious phenomenon from such similar or neighboring phenomena as purely moral or aesthetic sentiment. ... the very movement itself of the soul, putting itself in a personal relation of contact with the mysterious power of which it feels the presence, - it may be even before it has a name by which to call it. Wherever this interior prayer is lacking, there is no religion' (James, W., 1982, p.464). But can it be said that shamans pray in any conventional sense of the word? Does negotiating with the spirits consist of prayer? It is highly unlikely that most people would answer these questions in the affirmative and so this would seem to be an unsatisfactory definition too.

A 'functional' definition of religion centres on what it does for its followers, rather than what may exist in a supernatural realm, the way in which it enables its followers to come to terms with key events in their lives. Another approach to defining religion is to consider the characteristic forms religion takes, which is what Ninian Smart does. He considers that most religions have six main dimensions: the experiential, the mythic, the doctrinal, the ethical, the ritual, and the social/instructional (Smart, N.,1998). From this Chryssides concludes that 'a group of people can be said to constitute 'a religious group if they operate functionally as a religion – that is to say, if they offer a means of coping with the key events and the adversities and misfortunes of life, using the key characteristics of religious practice which are identified by scholars such as Smart' (Chryssides, G. D., 1999, pp.14-15). However, whether such people wish to regard themselves as a religious group or not is another matter.

'The belief in the transformation of human beings into animals and animals into human beings was a specific construction of the shaman. In fact the shaman was believed to possess this power. The ordinary man ... was fundamentally uninterested in such questions and accepted the interpretations of the shaman in his capacity as formulator just as he accepted the fact that the shaman alone possessed the power of transforming himself into an animal' (Radin, P., 1957, p.206). It can thus be seen that shamanism was never actually practised by the layman so the case for regarding it as a religion is far from convincing. As Eliade points out, 'wherever the immediate fate of the soul is not at issue, wherever there is no question of sickness (= loss of the soul) or death, or of misfortune, or of a great sacrificial rite involving some ecstatic experience … the shaman is not indispensable [to the shamanist as] a large part of religious life takes place without him' (Eliade, M., 1989, p.8). However, a case could be made for regarding both shamanism and neo-shamanism as a way of life – as is proposed by present-day practitioners such as Horwitz – this construction makes it possible for people of any religious persuasion to make use of the techniques.

The fact that shamanism can be practised alongside other religious beliefs in the manner described in the following quote, gives further support to the case for regarding shamanism to be more a way of life than a distinct religion:

> [In the case of the Kazak-Kirgiz baqca, the shamanic séance] begins with an invocation to Allah and the Moslem saints, and continues with an appeal to the jinni and threats to the evil spirits. The baqca sings on and on. At a certain moment the spirits take possession of him, and during this trance he "walks barefoot over red-hot iron" and several times introduces a lighted wick into his mouth. He touches the red-hot iron with his tongue and "with a knife, sharp as a razor, strikes at his face, leaving no visible mark." After these shamanic exploits he again invokes Allah: "O God, bestow happiness! Oh, deign to look on my tears! I implore thy help! …" Invocation of the Supreme God is not incompatible with shamanic healing, and we shall find it again among some peoples of extreme northeastern Siberia. But among the Kazak-Kirgiz first place is given to expelling the evil spirits that have taken possession of the patient. To accomplish this,

25

the baqca puts himself in the shamanic state, that is, obtains insensibility to fire and knife cuts, in other words, assumes the condition of a "spirit"; as such, he has the power to frighten and expel the demons of disease (Eliade, M., 1989, pp.219-220. The quotes are taken from "Magie et exorcisme chez les Kazak-Kirghizes et autres peoples turcs orientaux," by J. Castagne).

To summarize all the different arguments, and to present as clear a definition as is possible given all the difficulties that have been outlined above, the last word on the complex issue that has been explored in this chapter is left to Jeannette Gagan:

> Devoid of conventional trappings of religion as we know it, shamanism has no catalog of doctrines or index of moral declarations, no buildings honouring its deities, no prayer assignments for congregants, and no hierarchy of power. Nor does it impart devotion to a messianic cause. What it does impart is a belief in many gods and spirits, as well as faith in the actions and narratives inspired by this belief. Can such a grounding be called "religious"? According to university religion professor Ake Hultkrantz, it can. "Since the supernatural world is the world of religion," he states, "shamanism plays a religious role." Amid the recent upsurge of interest in shamanism, a more secularized interpretation of its practices has emerged, including that of Hungarian researcher Mihaly Hoppal: 'Shamanism is a complex system of beliefs which includes the knowledge of and belief in the names of helping spirits in the shamanic pantheon, the memory of certain texts (sermons, shaman-songs, legends, myths, etc.), the rules for activities (rituals, sacrifices, the technique of ecstasy, etc.) and the objects, tools and paraphernalia used by shamans (drum, stick, bow, mirror, costumes, etc.). All these components are closely connected by beliefs given in the shamanic complex ... [Shamanism is] an overtly altruistic ideology which, in our egoistic and materialistic times, contains a decisively positive program for

life' [Mihaly Hoppal, 1987, p.95]. Hence it appears that shamanism both is and is not a religion. It stands apart from institutionalized religion, yet participates in an ancient mystical tradition that author John Lash describes as "perhaps the oldest form of practical spirituality in the world" (Gagan, J. M., 1998, pp.22-23).

Neo-Shamanism

The current appeal of New Age beliefs and practices has encouraged a similar, if more exclusive, market for 'Neo-Shamanism', as individuals and groups in contemporary Western society adapt what they take to be exotic shamanistic lore for ritual healing and other spiritual purposes (Lewis, 2003, p.ix).

Rowena Pattee defines a neo-shaman as 'a modern person whose experiences of dying to the limited self and of the resultant ecstasy lead to self-empowerment and sacrifice for the benefit of his or her community' (Doore, G. (Ed.), 1988, p.17). And as Joan Townsend explains in the same volume, neo-shamanism blends portions of specific shamanic traditions of different societies around the world into a new complex of beliefs and practices (*Ibid.* p.74).

> The shaman is indispensable in any ceremony that concerns the experiences of the human soul [when it is seen as] ... a precarious psychic unit, inclined to forsake the body and an easy prey for demons and sorcerers. [This is because] he commands the techniques of ecstasy – ... his soul can safely abandon his body and roam at vast distances, can penetrate the underworld and rise to the sky. Through his own ecstatic experience he knows the roads of the extraterrestrial regions. He can go below and above because he has already been there. The danger of losing his way in these forbidden regions is still great; but sanctified by his initiation and furnished with his guardian spirits, the shaman is the only human being able to challenge the danger and venture into a mystical geography (Eliade, M., 1964, p.182).

In the case of neo-shamanism, however, the training is designed so that the shamanists are instructed in the techniques of ecstasy by means of which they are empowered to help themselves, and this is the main difference between the old and the new.

> In traditional forms of shamanism, shamanists only occasionally practise as shamans, among the Chukchee for example: 'During the ceremonies celebrated by the head of the family, everyone, even the children, takes a try at the drum. This is the case, for example, on the occasion of the "autumn slaughter," when animals are immolated to ensure a supply of game throughout the year. The drum is beaten – for each family has its own drum – and attempts are made to incarnate the "spirits" and to shamanize. ... The ceremony is held in the outer tent and by day, whereas shamanic séances take place in the sleeping room, at night, and in complete darkness. One after the other, the members of the family imitate "possession by the spirits" in shamanic fashion, writhing, leaping into the air, and trying to emit inarticulate sounds, which are supposed to be the voice and language of the "spirits." Sometimes even, shamanic cures are attempted and prophecies are uttered, to which no one pays attention. (Eliade, M., 1964, p.253).

However, such instances of "family shamanism" seem to be few and far between and can be regarded, in the words of Eliade, as nothing more than 'a plagiaristic aping of the ecstatic techniques of the professional shaman' (*Ibid.* p.253).

A characteristic of neo-shamanism is that the beliefs of the practitioners are much more eclectic than those of the classic shaman. 'The fundamental assumption that all things are connected leads to a heavily ecological focus ... that reminds one of the earlier hippie beliefs, and a serious concern for the survival of the earth and the environment' (Doore, G. (Ed.), 1988, p.80). The expensive 'crash courses' they tend to offer have come in for a lot of criticism from purists. However, Michael Harner has countered such criticisms of his teaching with the following argument: 'If the nation states of the world are working day and night on a crash course of their own for our mutual annihilation, we cannot afford to be any slower in our work in the opposite direction' (*Ibid.* p.81). This argument was particularly pertinent as it came just after the nuclear accident at Chernobyl nuclear plant in 1986.

Neo-shamanism includes Celtic Shamanism as practised and taught by people such as Caitlin Matthews, Core Shamanism practised and taught by people such as Michael Harner and Sandra Ingermann who run the Foundation for Shamanic Studies in America, and the anthropologist Jonathan Horwitz who runs the Scandinavian Centre for Shamanic Studies Northern Europe. In this country centres such as Eagle's Wing Centre for Contemporary Shamanism, founded by Leo Rutherford, cater for the ever-growing interest in the subject. Core Shamanism can be described as being based on indigenous shamanism, but stripped of elements specific to particular cultures.

John and Caitlin Matthews, in their own words, are

respected initiators in the Celtic and Arthurian traditions, and have opened many doors to a re-appreciation of our ancestral and mythic heritage. They are the authors of over 70 books. John's best-loved works are *The Celtic Shaman, Healing the Wounded King* and *The Winter Solstice*. Caitlín's books include *Singing the Soul Back Home, Celtic Devotional, and Sophia, Goddess of Wisdom*. They are the joint authors of *The Western Way, The Encyclopedia of Celtic Wisdom*, and *The Arthurian Tarot*. Their books have been translated into many languages including French, Italian, German, Czech, Dutch, Hebrew, Japanese and Russian. The material in these books is based upon practical knowledge which they teach worldwide. Together they have pioneered the shamanic use of the vatic and spiritual elements within ancestral and Celtic traditions, and are co-founders of The Foundation of Inspirational and Oracular Studies. They have made numerous appearances on TV in UK and US, and have been advisers on several series ... They live in Oxford where

Caitlín has a shamanic practice dedicated to midwifing the soul. (from their website: www.hallowquest.org accessed on 28/7/04).

According to a video and audio recordings produced for the Open University course AD317, Caitlin describes herself as practising Celtic Shamanism. I would have nothing to quibble about if she were to call herself a Core shamanic counsellor, in other words a practitioner who takes universal elements that can be found in all forms of shamanism and incorporates them into an eclectic approach that is adapted to suit clients in the 21st century. The problem for me is the use of the word Celtic. It is unlikely that there is any way of verifying whether what she does is actually authentic or not, or whether it has its foundation in traditional practices. On one of the cassettes that accompany the course, *Audio 3*, she acknowledges the problem when she proposes that tradition is flexible and that if it doesn't work then it has to change. Yet surely, once it is changed it is no longer tradition: so this argument just does not work for me. It also removes some of the credibility from what she is purporting to practise. Tradition can be regarded as 'the creation of the future out of the past', and history can be viewed as 'an artful assembly of materials from the past, designed for usefulness in the future' (Glassie, 1995, p.395).

Matthews does make the valid point that 'we live in a society that has become spiritually and esoterically illiterate. People no longer trust the signs their instincts, visions and dreams show them … People want to be connected to their ancient past,' (*op.cit.*). Shamanic practices, whether their origins are genuinely Celtic or taken from other sources, would seem to satisfy this need. She also offers a possible justification for one of the more controversial practices – the use of divination – by asking whether it is merely fortune-telling or questioning the gods through the signs the Universe provides us, tuning in to the 'other world', the world we don't see as well as the world we see. Such an interpretation allows people to reconcile the conflict between rationalism and the concept of divine intervention, by promoting the idea that religion is not about belief but about learning to read the signs to enter a world of knowledge, rather like observation in a scientific experiment.

On the video that accompanies the OU Course, *Video 5*, Matthews presents a demonstration of what she calls Celtic Divination. However, it is highly doubtful whether what she practises has much to do with the Celts. She encourages the client to formulate her own question and says she will leave it to her to interpret the answer, which could well be a technique taken from a training manual for person-centred therapists. However, she then fails to put her words into practice, interpreting the journey herself: 'which said you have a very strong vocation ... as though part of what you've been pursuing you have been aware of ... going in the same direction of others of your kind.' It thus becomes a disempowering rather than an empowering experience for the client, defeating the whole purpose of the exercise. She also makes use of 'healing songs', citing her own short-sightedness as one of the reasons for this practice. However, once again where is the evidence to suggest there is anything particularly Celtic about this?

The religions that adapt effectively to the world we live in are those which use resources that are unsponsored by an inherited structure and have the ability to jump across cultural frontiers. Matthews is certainly jumping across cultures but the problem is that she is not really acknowledging this is what she is doing as long as she persists in using the word Celtic to describe what she does.

When Matthews attempts to support her case by referring to our knowledge of the past, holes can easily be found in her argument. For example, in *Religion Today: A*

Reader, she asserts that 'Samhain and Beltain were the two major festivals, since they marked the division of the year into two parts: Winter and Summer. Both Festivals were considered to be the prime time to communicate with the Otherworld. The doors of the sidhe were thought to be open on these nights. The feast of Oimelc marked the loosening of Winter's grip and Lughnasadh marked the gathering together of the tribe at high summer' (Mumm, S.,(ed),2002). However, as Hutton points out in the same volume, 'the notion of a distinctive "Celtic" ritual year, with four festivals at the quarter-days and an opening at Samhain, is a scholastic construction of the eighteenth and nineteenth centuries which should now be considerably revised or even abandoned altogether.' James is similarly dismissive of some of the bogus claims made: '"The Celts" must be rejected as an ethnic label for the populations of the islands during the Iron Age, the Roman period or indeed medieval times, not least in the direct sense that they did not use this name for themselves. The name is also to be rejected in the more general sense, in that it implies that culturally the Iron Age populations of Ireland and Britain were all the same kind of people and that they were all essentially the same as the continental Celts.' (James, W., 1982). I am not for one instant doubting Matthew's sacred intent or suggesting that the rituals she practises and teaches are of dubious spiritual benefit. However, I am questioning the label she has attached to them.

As Smart points out in *The World's Religions*, 'Western Europe is a consumerist entity. Choices have rarely been so abundant. And something similar is beginning to happen in religion; a kind of consumerism, with many new varieties being added as cultures cross and merge. There is a tendency for individuals to make up their own religions. This often means that they are serious about spirituality, but not about tradition,' as is evident from the sloppy research that is used to support the claims made by certain 'New Age' or Pagan practitioners.

'God is real for Christians whether or not he exists' (Smart, 1973, p.54). In the same way, experiences of non-ordinary reality are real for shamanic practitioners and it is certainly not my purpose to devalue them. It is the trend towards individuals 'customizing' their own religions that I am commenting on and Mathews's version of Celtic shamanism provides a good example of this. It can be seen that religion and its associated rituals can sometimes be nothing more than an act of interpretation based on evidence that may well be inaccurate and unsubstantiated.

'Globalization' is a term used to describe the 'development of social and economic relationships stretching worldwide', the effect of which is that 'many aspects of people's lives are influenced by organizations and social networks located thousands of miles away from the societies in which they live' (Giddens, 1993, p.742). 'National boundaries, cultural traditions and individual identities can be challenged or superseded by these globalizing tendencies' (Bowman, M., Herbert, D. & Mumm, S. ,2001, pp.70-71). A good example of this is the Native American practices that have been taken up by people in Europe, in a milieu far removed from the setting in which they were created.

A feature of contemporary religion is the way people are turning to religious movements that enable them to side with the 'innocent' in the face of disillusionment with the state of world. Identifying with a people perceived to have been oppressed allows one to say 'not guilty' of the oppression. 'Being Celtic, [for example,] not only allows one to be 'not English'; it allows one to be 'not British' (with all the attendant imperial baggage), 'not like the mainstream', 'not exploiter' of either other peoples or the environment; in short, 'not guilty' (Pearson, J., (ed.), 2002, p.96). The same refuge can be found within American Indian spirituality. As Vine Deloria Jr.

explains in *Religion Today*, 'today it is popular to be an Indian. Within a decade it may be a necessity: people are not going to want to take the blame for the sorry state of the nation, and claiming allegiance with the most helpless racial minority may well be the way to escape accusations'.

In the article by Jung in *Religion Today: A Reader*, religion is defined as

> A careful and scrupulous observation of what Rudolf Otto aptly termed numinosum – a dynamic agency or effect not caused by an arbitrary act of will. On the contrary, it seizes and controls the human subject, who is always rather its victim than its creator. A great many ritualistic performances are carried out for the sole purpose of producing at will the effect of the numinosum by means of certain devices of a magical nature, such as invocation, incantation, sacrifice, meditation and other yoga practices, self-inflicted tortures of various descriptions, and so forth. (Mumm,S.(Ed),2002)

All three of the Native American rituals described below produce just such an effect. Moreover, so powerful can the effect of the numinosum be that it could even be said to have an addictive quality, which goes a long way to explaining its attraction:

> The Sweat Lodge is a domed structure built of saplings and covered with skins ... Heated stones are placed in it, and the water poured on them turns to steam. The sweating of the participant revitalizes his spirit. He may also be visited by supernaturals and given visions which provide clues to communal and individual concerns. The Vision Quest entails a person staying on a hillside in a shallow hole for a few days, without food or water. The quest is for a vision, which is then interpreted for him by a medicine man on his return. The Sun Dance ceremony involves cutting a tree and using it as the central pole of a lodge representing the universe. During a whole day the dancers move around the periphery

gazing at the Sun as continuously as possible. Some pierce themselves with hooks which are tied to the central tree and planted in their chests. They are encouraged by the martial sons and drumbeats of the musicians. The dancers bind themselves to the heart of the cosmic mystery, in preparation for the great midsummer hunts which will replenish the food and life of the whole group. (Smart, N., 1998, Second Edition).

Apparently 'there are now Druidic sweat lodges ... opinions vary as to whether this is justified "revival"', creative borrowing and respectful enhancement of one native tradition by reference to another, or rather dubious cultural theft' (Pearson, J., (ed.), 2002, p.83). Mumm quotes a Lakota Elder who points out, 'Each people have their own ways. You cannot mix these ways together, because each people's ways are balanced' (Matthew King, a Lakota elder, cited in Churchill, 1991,p.14). However, 'Sun Bear, like many others who popularize indigenous traditions among a Euro-American audience, contends that his activities are legitimate precisely because they are synchronistic: they are derived from a variety of tribes and some elements, such as crystal healing, are not derived from First Nations' practices' (Pearson, J., (ed.) ,2002, p.113). It can be argued that one of the causes of cultural appropriation is a deep spiritual hunger that does not appear to be satisfied within the religions that the Euro-American consumers of such alternatives are born into.

> Inspiration for ritual is drawn from ancient pasts (e.g. Celtic, Egyptian and Greek civilization) discovered through archaeology, classics, myth and history, or from indigenous peoples ... [and] practices and beliefs are revived and recreated to fit the context of modern day life. Some practitioners also use ideas and concepts developed by Jung to add another level of meaning to their rituals. (Pearson, J., (ed.), 2002, p.4).

There is a 'real danger in assuming that human social life is best understood in terms of cognition and reason, leaving aside intuition, affect, transcendent experience, and the like. Those omissions seem particularly serious when it comes to religion' (Ammerman, 1997 pp.119-120). One of the reasons why the practice of rituals so appeals to people is that it can provide the opportunity for such experiences. Moreover, 'since the borrowing of myth, symbol, and rite from one group by another is a central characteristic of cultural and religious evolution, it is inappropriate for religious studies scholars to categorically condemn such developments' (Taylor, 1997, p.184). In fact, 'it may be reasonable to argue that religious change is inevitable, and that attempting to preserve a tradition for its 'own' may instead fossilize it' (Pearson, J., (ed.), 2002, p.127). Even so, what has been borrowed should be acknowledged as such, and not passed off as something it is clearly not.

Centres for the teaching and practice of neo-shamanism are being set up all the time and this is not the place to provide a comprehensive list of what is available. However, three organisations can be recommended.

The Foundation for Shamanic Studies was established by internationally renowned anthropologist Michael Harner

> with a three-fold mission to study, to teach, and to preserve shamanism, the Foundation for Shamanic Studies has built a reputation of consistency and dependability by providing reliable training in Core Shamanism to interested learners worldwide. Dr. Harner has been recognized as a pioneer in the field of anthropology and shamanism since the early 60's when he chose to immerse himself in tribal spiritual traditions rather than restrict his study to more traditional academic techniques. (www. shamanism.org, accessed 29 July 2004)

According to the site statistics, more than 5,000 people each year follow their training in core shamanism, described as 'the near universal methods of shamanism without a specific cultural perspective', and 200-plus training programs are given each year in North America, Europe, Latin America and Australia.

'In sociological terms, there is a tendency towards "institutionalization"; what starts out as a loosely organized movement, often centred around a charismatic leader, becomes a structured organization with clearly defined tenets, rituals and criteria for determining who belong and who do not' (Chrysiddes, G.D., 1999, p.17). A good example of how this works in practice can be seen from the way in which Core Shamanic Counsellors who have trained with the Scandinavian Centre for Shamanic Studies are not recognized by the Foundation for Shamanic Studies even though the courses run by the two organizations are more or less identical.

The books of Carlos Castaneda (describing his apprenticeship to a Yaqui shaman-sorcerer, Don Juan, in northern Mexico) whether or not they are entirely genuine, have proved to be valuable teaching stories for many people and have served to arouse greater interest in shamanism. However, Michael Harner, probably more than any other one person, has shown through his writing and workshops, how shamanism can be applied today in practice. Moreover, the Foundation for Shamanic Studies, which was founded by Harner, has done a great deal both to fund research and to support the few remaining aboriginal shamans whose traditional lifestyles are under threat in the face of so-called 'progress'. An example of this is the way in which the Foundation has helped fund the main organisation overseeing the revival of shamanism in Tuva.

To fully understand the nature of neo-shamanism as it has developed in Siberia, it is necessary to know something of the background to the current situation. As Vitebsky explains,

'The Communist regimes of the 20th century covered much of the heartland of Asian shamanism, which was persecuted along with the region's many other religions. Since there were no shamanist temples to pull down, persecution was aimed directly at the shamans themselves' (Vitebsky, P., 2001, p.136). Under Communism, shamanic practices were actively discouraged. A Tuvan called Gendos was recruited as part of the propaganda machine and this is how he describes the role he was required to play:

> Towards the end of my time at school I performed on stage in front of various dignitaries – that is, for the Party. I played the part of a kham, and up there on the stage I had to hide behind a drum, then jump out, dance a bit as if around a fire, and then chuck my drum to one side and the drumstick to the other – as if I was throwing it all away. Then I had to wrench off my shamanic cloak, revealing Party Youth clothes underneath. The final part of my act was to jump up and down on the kham garments, dirtying them on the stage. "The Last Shaman", my performance was called. (Allen, B., 2000, p.81).

Nevertheless, people's belief in the khams somehow survived and they were helped to revive shamanic practices after the fall of Communism by benefactors such as Michael Harner.

However, '… with the collapse of the Soviet empire, there'd also been a collapse in infrastructure. We passed through the open market – and learnt that many of the women behind the stalls used to be teachers, who'd had to give it up because they were never paid' (*Ibid*, p.71). Consequently, earning enough to make ends meet became the main concern of most people, and helps to explain why the neo-shamanic movement is so concerned with making money. Although the picture of Kenin-Lopsam painted by Benedict Allen is far from complimentary, it is hardly surprising given the circumstances:

> ... a Living Treasure of Shamanism. That was what the sign
> at the museum said, noting the visiting fee to see him was
> ten roubles. ... The title was bequeathed by Michael Harner
> (*Ibid.* p.91).

To interview and film in the Dungur Centre, Benedict Allen
was not only required to make a hefty donation, but also to
give Kenin-Lopsan '"something for himself" ... a $50 dollar
note - the equivalent of almost a month's wage for ordinary
Tuvans' (*Ibid.* p.95).

Despite the financial temptations that characters such
as Kenin-Lapsam would seem to have succumbed to, this does
not imply the neo-shamans in Tuva are necessarily charlatans.
There are good and bad shamans, just as there are good and
bad priests, and there probably always will be.

It is interesting to note that in the Jivaro Indian tribe of
South America, among whom Michael Harner carried out
some of his research, would-be shamans select themselves and
established practitioners sell them their knowledge. As Roger
Walsh points out, tongue-in-cheek, this is 'a practice
enthusiastically followed by today's Western shamans in their
weekend workshops' (Walsh, 1990, p.39). Although it is
undoubtedly true that some practitioners unethically exploit
the fashionable interest in shamanism, it would be unfair to tar
everyone with the same brush, and people like Harner deserve
to be taken seriously as they can be seen to be doing a lot of
good work.

It might come as a surprise to some that neo-
shamanism can also refer to the revival (in an adapted form) by
aboriginal peoples of practices that have fallen into disuse,
such as the Spirit Lodge Ceremony among the Arapaho
Indians witnessed and recorded by Hultrantz in August 1955.
'The acting medicine-man was an Oglala Sioux from the Pine
Ridge Reservation in South Dakota by the name of Mark Big
Road [and] all conversation during the performance was held

in English, since Mark, being a Sioux, does not understand the Arapaho language' (Edsman, C.M. (ed.), 1967, p.38). It can be seen from accounts like this that the revival of Tuvan shamanism is far from being a unique occurrence.

Among his other achievements, Michael Harner can be credited with having developed a way of using shamanic techniques in the field of counselling. In his own words,

> Harner Method Shamanic Counseling, is a system for permitting clients to make their own shamanic journeys of divination to nonordinary reality, where they personally obtain direct spiritual wisdom and guidance in answer to the questions most important in their lives. ... One of the main features of shamanic counselling, however, is to turn this procedure around so that the client is being counselled to become his or her own shaman for this type of journey. The object of this change is to restore spiritual power and authority to the client (Doore, G. (Ed.), 1988, p.179).

> The use of a drumming tape [played through a set of earphones] ... permits the shamanic counsellor to utilize ... the technique of *simultaneous narration*, wherein the client is asked to narrate out loud [into a lapel microphone connected to a recorder] the details of his or her journey as it is happening (Ibid. p.180).[1]

---

[1] It is perhaps worth mentioning at this point that there is an element of doubt as to whether the drumming is actually responsible for inducing an altered state of consciousness: 'Drumming has been central to neo-shamanic movements, where a pulse of approximately 200 beats a minute is said to enable many inexperienced people to enter an ASC quite rapidly. The rhythms which produce a trance among shamans, however, are found elsewhere without having any effect. Indeed, when a shaman performs, the other people present hear the same rhythm but do not fall into a trance unless it is expected of them. ... It seems that while music and dance can have powerful effects, they do not so much induce trance as organize it in relation to a belief system. Listeners must also make their own psychic contribution' (Vitebsky, P., 2001, p.81).

The recording makes it possible to carry out an immediate review and analysis of the experience and of the information gained. Harner regards the system as 'a method of personal empowerment wherein one comes to acquire respect for one's own ability to obtain spiritual wisdom without relying on external mediators. The whole idea is to return to people what was once taken away from them when state began perpetuating monopolies on access to spiritual knowledge' (*Ibid.* p.181). Workshops and courses providing training in this method are given by the Foundation for Shamanic Studies in its Shamanic Counseling Training programs.

Sandra Ingermann, who works with Michael Harner, specializes in utilizing the technique of soul retrieval as a form of therapy. In her own words: 'With this method, the shamanic practitioner retrieves any life essence that has been lost by a client due to an emotional or physical trauma. Loss of a part of the soul can create an "opening" in a person where an illness might enter. ... It is the role of the shaman to track down that person's soul or essence later in non-ordinary reality and physically return it to the body' (Ingermann, S., 1993, p.23).

To give you some idea of what the process entails, here are a couple of extracts from an account of the procedure:

> For a soul retrieval, I will ask Anne to let down next to me on my rug in the small room in which I work. I will touch her at the shoulder, hip, and ankle so that the psychic connection between the two of us is strong. I use a tape of drumming so that my own free soul can leave my body and search for Anne's soul. (Ingermann, S., 1993, p.25).

> I pulled that part from nonordinary reality into ordinary reality and proceeded to blow the soul back into Anne's heart center and then, after sitting her up, into the crown of her head. (*Ibid.* p.29).

The process does not end at this point because it is re-enforced with follow-up work: 'Once the healing is performed, the next step is for the client to start to look at life after illness, a process that involves two very crucial questions: What changes do I need to create in my life that will keep me healthy? How do I want to use my creative energy to make something positive in my life?' (*Ibid*. p.35).

The second organisation I will mention is the **Scandinavian Center for Shamanic Studies**, this, in the words of its founders,

> is a small independent network, started by Jonathan Horwitz and Annette Høst, founded on teaching and encouraging the practice of shamanism. The Center is a center in the spiritual sense of the word, as the fire in the center of a council circle, as the center of the circles of ripples in a still pond after a pebble has been tossed. It is here ideas are born, and our activities are coordinated, but our courses are held in various locations in Europe and occasionally in North America. We started in 1986 when Jonathan taught his first introductory workshop. Our courses are centered on learning to use the ritual tools of shamanism, experiencing shamanism as a spiritual path, shamanic healing, and embracing the Circle and all of Nature. Jonathan Horwitz has studied and worked with shamanism since 1972. For eight years he was on the staff of The Foundation for Shamanic Studies, USA. Jonathan has an M.A. in anthropology, and is a shamanic counselor (HMSC). He has taught courses in shamanism for the past fifteen years. Annette Høst has studied and practiced shamanism for more than fifteen years. Her teaching builds partly on her own research in Nordic Shamanism and the cycles of Nature. She has taught courses in shamanism since 1989. (www.shaman-center.dk)

Lastly, **Eagle's Wing Centre for Contemporary Shamanism** is based in London and was founded by Leo Rutherford. This is what Leo has to say about himself on his website:

> I worked in industry for twenty years, and for the last twelve years of that was a Managing Director of a manufacturing company which made tin cans and drums. By the age of forty, I was suffering from acute stress and depression and 'normal' life did not make sense to me any more. I took my life apart and set out to find an alternative path, a path with more heart. I went through all kinds of therapy, learned to dance, sing and play in a way I hadn't since childhood, and I gained my MA in Holistic Psychology at Antioch University in San Francisco, where I lived for five years. Quite unexpectedly I came across the beautiful ancient wisdom of the indigenous shamans. I was introduced to this path by Joan Halifax in 1980 and since then have continued to learn from a wide variety of teachers. As I have got older, so I have become younger! It is my great joy to pass on to others through these workshops, some of the experience and knowledge that has helped me to transform my life. A process that goes on and on... ... The work of Eagle's Wing is to help people connect their inner and outer worlds, to heal old wounds within, to become able to bring dreams from the world of spirit into matter and thus enjoy a creative and fruitful life *to dance their dreams awake* and to become a part of the solution instead of part of the problem of human life on Earth. (www.shamanism.co.uk)

Eleanor Ott, a contemporary American anthropologist, is extremely critical of the neo-shamanists. As the following quotation shows, she is clearly concerned that there is a danger that they may act irresponsibly: 'Without a community that recognizes the new shamans as an integral part of the culture, what makes these people in fact shamans at all except that they so call themselves?' (Narby, J., & Huxley, F., 2001, p.282).

Power is directed by the shaman's own inner will for evil or for good. In this sense, power itself is neutral and available to the shaman who shapes power by his own, by her own intention, desire, motive, drive, and will. Especially for the new shaman isolated from a watchful community, it is more difficult to remain pure in heart with regard to issues of power (*Ibid*. p.283).

Perhaps the new shamans should consider whether it is important or appropriate in any way to call themselves shamans in order to practice whatever techniques they have mastered for the benefit of others. For some few perhaps who are willing and able to make the lifetime commitment to the discipline that is required, it is appropriate. But for most others, the mantle of the shaman is only a veneer, an outer covering, which they put on and take off as convenient. Better, and more honest, to think of themselves, and call themselves by some other name than by the name that carries with it the weight and responsibility of shaman (*Ibid*. p.284).

Although the points Ott makes have some validity, it has to be remembered there have always been both 'good' and 'bad' shamans, just as there are good and bad people in every profession and there probably always will be.

As Maddox points out, 'Of the twelve original apostles one was a traitor. There are many insincere clergymen; there are many quack doctors; but in either case the greater number of clergymen and doctors are reliable and trustworthy men' (Maddox, J. L., 2003, p.105). 'That medicine men in the capacity of physician generally learn their profession in good faith, and retain their belief until the last, is evidenced by the fact that when they fall ill or are in straits, they solicit assistance of others in the same profession. A case in point is the Dieyerie tribes of South America, whose shamans, when they are themselves sick, call in other medicine men to wait upon them' (*Ibid.* p.111).

The fact that there have always been both 'good' and 'bad' shamans can also be backed up with the following account that Rasmussen obtained from a Caribou-Eskimo shaman:

> "We shamans of the interior," said the old man, "have no special sprit language and believe that the real shamans do not need it. On my travels I have sometimes been present at a séance among the saltwater dwellers. These shamans never seem trustworthy to me. It always appeared to me that they attached more weight to tricks that would astonish the audience, when they jumped about the floor and lisped all sorts of absurdities and lies in their so-called spirit language; to me all this seemed only amusing and as something that would impress the ignorant. A real shaman does not jump about the floor and do tricks, nor does he seek help by the aid of darkness, by putting out the lamps, to make the minds of his neighbours uneasy. For myself, I do not think that wisdom or knowledge about things that are hidden can be sought in that manner. True wisdom is only to be found far away from the people, out in the great solitude, and it is not found in play but only through suffering. Solitude and suffering open the human mind, and therefore a shaman must seek his wisdom there." (K. Rasmussen, 1921-1924, vol. VII, No. 2, pp. 54-55).

Roger Walsh echoes the sentiments of the anthropologist Eleanor Ott:

> It is a matter of debate ... whether a Westerner who uses shamanic practices divorced from the social, cultural, and mythological setting in which they were originally embedded can usefully be called a shaman. (Walsh, 1990, p.266)

46

The title of 'shaman' has never been a label that a person would traditionally apply to themselves. It would depend very much on whether they were judged to be effective practitioners by the people who turned to them for help. Consequently, a more appropriate definition for such people might be 'neo-shamanic practitioners'. However, it has to be said nobody who has worked with practitioners such as Michael Harner or Jonathan Horwitz, as I have been fortunate enough to be able to do, would be likely to hesitate when it came to calling them shamans.

A word of warning might be appropriate at this point for any reader looking for a neo-shamanic teacher to work with. 'Those who approach spiritual teachers tend to be seekers who suffer from unhappiness and hope to overcome it. More than that, they typically expect the teacher to alleviate their suffering. They look on him or her as a shaman, a miracle worker, a soul doctor to whom they must surrender in childlike fashion to be miraculously made whole. This hope is utterly misplaced. Genuine teachers will always do their utmost to destroy the disciple's mental image of them as omnipotent and omniscient father or mother figures' (Feurstein, G., 1991, p.121). If the person you choose to be your teacher does not have this aim, it is highly unlikely that he/she is genuine and the advice is to be on your guard.

According to Vitebsky, 'The shaman's experience is never just a personal voyage of discovery, but also a service to the community' (Vitebsky, P., 2001, p.96). He later reinforces the point by adding that 'The shaman is not a private mystic, but exists to serve a community' (*Ibid* p.110). However, it has to be pointed out that in neo-shamanism, this is not always the case. A lot of people learn how to 'journey' solely for purposes of self development and may have no interest in serving a community unless it is a drumming circle to which they may belong. Others, once they have learned the techniques, may decide to practise them entirely on their own regardless of what the intention of their trainers might have been.

To conclude this chapter, I would like now like to turn to the question of how we can account for the appeal of neo-shamanism. This is what Joan B Townsend has to say on the subject:

> The people who are drawn to these neo-shamanic associations are often disenchanted with traditional religions and often with much of Western society. Although they tend not to be affiliated with any organized religion, they all continue intensive personal quests for spirituality, meaning and transcendence. They are searching for new ways to organize their lives in a more satisfying manner and hoping to find more meaning in the religious and philosophical sense. They remain "religious" in the broad meaning of the term and retain their beliefs in some form of supernatural God-like being or Consciousness (Doore, G. (Ed.), 1988, p.78).

> Shamanism possesses important mystical truths and the potential for transcendent experiences for which so many people in Western society are desperately searching (*Ibid.* p.82).

One of the main reasons for the appeal of neo-shamanism, as Michael Harner points out, is that 'most persons can achieve in a few hours experiences that might otherwise take them years of silent meditation, prayer, or chanting. For this reason alone, shamanism is ideally suited to the contemporary life of busy people' (Harner, M., 1990 Third Edition, p. xii). It is worth noting that, for the same reason, so is the short story. People today are turning away from traditional forms of religion in search of alternatives and there are a number of reasons for this. Jung encapsulated one of the most important ones:

There is in the psyche a process that seeks its own goal independently of external factors. ... If the supreme value (Christ) and the supreme negation (sin) are outside, then the soul is void: its highest and lowest are missing. ... If the soul no longer has any part to play, religious life congeals into externals and formalities. ... In an outward form of religion where all the emphasis is on the outward figure (hence where we are dealing with a more or less complete projection), the archetype is identical with externalized ideas but remains unconscious as a psychic factor. When an unconscious content is replaced by a projected image to that extent, it is cut off from all participation in and influence on the conscious mind. (Jung, C.G., 1968 2nd Edition, pp.5-11).

The result of this is that

Far too many people are incapable of establishing a connection between the sacred figures and their own psyche: they cannot see to what extent the equivalent images are lying dormant in their own unconscious (*Ibid*. p.13).

It is for this reason that people today are turning to alternatives such as neo-shamanism and this factor goes a long way to explaining the growing popularity of such movements.

It is a truism that anything known becomes so familiar and hackneyed by frequent use that it gradually loses its meaning and hence its effect; whereas anything strange and unknown, and so completely different in its nature, can open doors hitherto locked and new possibilities of understanding (Jung, C.G., 1977, p.698).

The neo-shamanic movement that has sprung up in recent times can be seen to be doing just that.

According to Joseph Campbell, 'every one of the great traditions is today in profound disorder. What have been taught as their basic truths seem no longer to hold. Yet there is a great religious fervour and ferment evident among not only young people but old and middle-aged as well. The fervour, however, is in a mystical direction, and the teachers who seem to be saying most to many are those who have come to us from a world that was formerly regarded as having been left altogether behind in the great press forward of modern civilization, representing only archaic, outlived manners of thinking' (Campbell, J., 1973, pp.86-87). Campbell then goes on to refer to gurus from India, roshis from Japan, and lamas from Tibet. However, his analysis can surely be applied just as well to the neo-shamanic practitioners who have been the subject of this chapter.

Perhaps the last word of all on this subject should go to Eliade as it seems to me that he really captures the reason for the appeal of shamanism in the following quote:

> What the shaman can do today *in ecstasy*, could, at the dawn of time, be done by all human beings *in concreto*; they went up to heaven and came down again without recourse to trance. Temporarily and for a limited number of persons – the shamans – ecstasy re-establishes the primordial condition of all mankind. In this respect, the mystical experience of the "primitives" is a return to origins, a reversion to the mystical age of the lost paradise. For the shaman in ecstasy, the bridge or the tree, the vine, the cord, and so on – which, *in illo tempore* [in those days], connected earth with heaven – once again, for the space of an instant, becomes a present reality (Eliade, M., 1964, p.486).

My own experience suggests that this is as true for neo-shamanic practitioners as it is for aboriginal shamans.

Shamanic Journeys - to the Lower World, Middle World and Upper World

Different types of shamanic journeys can be undertaken - to the Lower World where you can make contact with Power Animals and to the Upper World where you can meet your Sacred Teacher. Journeys are also undertaken to the Land of the Dead, where the shaman acts as a psychopomp – a conductor of souls. There are also journeys for the purpose of divination and journeys to carry out Soul Retrievals. In the words of Jeannette Gagan,

> Soul loss, like its psychological counterpart, "dissociation," implies a splitting off of parts of the psyche as a result of trauma. ... Viewed psychologically, dissociation is a defence mechanism causing threatening feelings, impulses, or thoughts to be cast into the unconscious portion of the psyche. From the shaman's perspective, these split-off parts live in another dimension – a "nonordinary" yet parallel reality – and are accessible to those familiar with its topography (Gagan, J. M., 1998, p.9).

As Sandra Ingermann explains, 'It ... sometimes happens that the soul is afraid to come back, especially if it is a part that was abused at an early age and doesn't know that it is safe to come back now. Or maybe the soul has actually been stolen. Another person may take a piece of our essence to remain in connection with us, or someone may try to steal our power or energy' (Ingermann, S., 1993, p.26).

According to Michael Harner, Middle-world journeys are particularly common in the near-Arctic areas of North America and Siberia. Here food supplies are precarious and migrating animal herds must be located. On the other hand, in neo-shamanic practices such as those taught by Harner or Horwitz, journeys are undertaken to the Middle World to see events that take place in this reality in their non-ordinary reality forms and to gain a greater insight into their nature. And this is what Sandra Ingermann has to say about the Middle World:

> In nonordinary reality, the Middle World comes closest to our ordinary reality. Here I see scenes that I would experience in my waking life, but I am in an altered state of consciousness when looking at them. ... Shamans usually travel to the Middle World to find lost and stolen objects. I also travel to the Middle World to speak to the spirit of a client who is in a coma or unconscious to get permission to do healing work on his or her behalf (Ingermann, S., 1993, p.172).

As Eliade explains,

> The "clashing of rocks," the "dancing reeds," the gates in the shape of jaws, the "two razor-edged restless mountains," the "two clashing icebergs," the "active door," the "revolving barrier," the door made of the two halves of the eagle's beak, and many more – all these are images used in myths and sagas to suggest the insurmountable difficulties of passage to the Other World. ... Although originally the Other World is the world after death, it finally comes to mean any transcendent state, that is, any mode of being inaccessible to fleshly man and reserved for "spirits" or for man as a spiritual entity. ... All these mythical images and folklore motifs of the dangerous passage and the paradoxical transfer express the necessity for a change in mode of being to make it possible to attain the world of spirit (Eliade, 1958, pp.64-65).

He continues,

> Ascent and flight are proofs par excellence of the divinization of man. The specialists in the sacred – medicine men, shamans, mystics – are above all men who are believed to fly up to Heaven, in ecstasy or even in the flesh ... The descent

to the Underworld and the ascent to Heaven obviously denote different religious experiences; but the two experiences spectacularly prove that he who has undergone them has transcended the secular condition of humanity and that his behaviour is purely that of a spirit (Eliade, 1958, p.78).

Here is an account of a neo-shamanic journey to the Lower World recorded by Sandra Ingermann, who works with the Foundation for Shamanic Studies that was established by Michael Harner:

> When Nancy returned for our next session, I explained the process of journeying. I told her that this work would give her access to her own helping spirits so she could answer questions in her life, thus giving her back the power to make decisions that would be beneficial for her. I told her that we would start by learning how to go to the Lower World to find out who her own power animal was at this time. The Lower World is just one of the territories in nonordinary reality and seems to be a good place to start people in their work with shamanic journeying.
>
> I drummed for Nancy to provide the path out of and back to her body. I gave her the usual instructions for entering the Lower World: I asked her to think about an opening in the earth that she could enter – someplace that she had actually seen before. In this way she would know whether she was in ordinary or nonordinary reality. I emphasized that shamanism is a discipline in which it is very important to know what world one is in at all times. So when one's starting place is in ordinary reality, it is very clear at both the start and the finish of the journey which reality one is in.
>
> Nancy asked me if there was anything to fear in the Lower World. I answered that she had full control of her actions in a journey and so if something frightened her, she could always confront her fear, move away from it, or come back at any time (Ingermann, 1993, p.69).

Ingermann goes on

> I asked her to lie down and put a bandana over her eyes to
> block out the light, for in shamanism we see in the dark. I
> also explained to Nancy that the words *shamanic seeing* didn't
> necessarily mean visual seeing, and I instructed her to open
> up to all the senses she might use to access information. As
> soon as she heard the drumming, she was to enter the
> opening into the earth she had chosen, go down her tunnel,
> and put out a very strong telepathic message for her power
> animal to be waiting for her on the other side.
> She was to ask her power animal a simple yes-or-no question
> to see how it communicated with her. Some power animals
> communicate telepathically, some show symbols as an
> answer, and others will take the journeyer somewhere to
> show the answer. Once Nancy understood her animal's form
> of communication, she could ask it any question she chose
> (Ibid. p.70).

The next account describes the initiation of an Eskimo
Shaman and provides a striking contrast to what preceded it:

> When I was to be a shaman, I chose suffering through the
> two things that are most dangerous to us humans, suffering
> through hunger and suffering through cold. First I hungered
> five days and was then allowed to drink a mouthful of warm
> water. The old ones say that only if the water is warm will
> Pinga and Hila notice the novice and help him. Thereafter I
> went hungry another fifteen days, and again was given a
> mouthful of warm water. After that I hungered for ten days,
> and then could begin to eat though it only had to be the sort
> of food on which there is never any taboo, preferably fleshy
> meat, and never intestines, head, heart, or other entrails nor
> meat that had been touched by wolf or wolverine while it lay
> in a cache. I was to keep this diet for five months, and then
> the next five months might eat everything; but after that I
> was again forced to eat the meat diet that is prescribed for all
> those who must do penance in order to become clean. The
> old ones attached great importance to the food that the

would-be shaman might eat. Thus a novice who wished to possess the ability to kill had never to eat [a specific kind of] salmon. If they eat it, they will, instead of killing others, kill themselves.

My instructor was my wife's father, Perqanaq. Perqanaq built a small snow hut at the place where I was to be, this snow hut being no bigger than that I could just get under cover and sit down. I was given no sleeping skin to protect me against the cold; only a little piece of caribou skin to sit upon. There I was shut in. The snow hut in which I sat was built far from the trails of men and when Perqanaq had found the spot where he thought it ought to be built, he stopped the little sledge at a distance and there I had to remain seated until the snow hut was ready. Not even I, who was after all the one to have to stay there, might set my footprints in the vicinity of the hut and old Perqanaq had to carry me from the sledge over to the hut so that I could crawl in. As soon as I had become alone Perqanaq enjoined me to think of one single thing and that was to draw Pinga's attention to the fact that there I sat and wished to be a shaman. Pinga should own me.

My novitiate took place in the middle of the coldest winter and I, who never got anything to warm me and must not move, was very cold, and it was so tiring having to sit without daring to lie down, that sometimes it was as if I had died a little. Only towards the end of the thirty days did a helping spirit come to me, a lovely and beautiful helping spirit, whom I had never thought of. It was a white woman. She came to me whilst I had collapsed, exhausted, and was sleeping. But still I saw her lifelike hovering over me, and from that day I could not close my eyes or dream without seeing her. There is this remarkable thing about my helping spirit, that I have never seen her while awake, but only in dreams. She came to me from Pinga and was a sign that Pinga had now noticed me and would give me powers that would make me a shaman.

When a new moon was lighted and had the same size as the one that had shone for us when we left the village, Perqanaq came again with his little sledge and stopped a long way from the snow hut. But by this time I was not very much alive any more and had not the strength to rise. In fact I could not stand on my feet. Perqanaq pulled me out of the hut and carried me down to the sledge and dragged me home in the same manner as he had dragged me to Kingarjuit. I was now so completely emaciated that the veins on my hands and body and feet had quite disappeared. For a long time I might only eat very little in order to again get my intestines extended, and later came the diet that was to help cleanse my body.

For a whole year I was not to lie with my wife, who, however, had to make my food. For a whole year I had to have my own little cooking pot and my own meat dish; no one else was allowed to eat of what had been cooked for me.

Later, when I had quite become myself again, I understood that I had become the shaman of my village, and it did happen that my neighbours or people from a long distance away called me to heal a sick person or to "inspect a course" if they were going to travel. When this happened, the people of my village were called together and I told them what I had been asked to do. Then I left the tent or snow house and went out into solitude, away from the dwellings of man. But those who remained behind had to sing continuously, just to keep themselves happy and lively.

These days of "seeking for knowledge" are very tiring, for one must walk all the time, no matter what the weather is like and only rest in short snatches. I am usually quite done up, tired, not only in body but also in head, when I have found what I sought. (K. Rasmussen, *op.cit.* 1921-1924, vol. VII, No. 2, pp. 52 ff).

As Georg Feurstein observes, 'All too often, especially in New Age circles, people are so fascinated with the idea that enlightenment lies in the pathless "here and now," that they remain deaf to the countless traditional tales of struggle engaged by spiritual practitioners prior to their awakening' (Feurstein, G., 1991, p.110).

Heelas maintains that 'the beliefs of the traditional (aboriginal) shaman – that there are upper and lower universes, for example – ... [can be] understood expressivistically and instrumentally. ... Rather than there actually being other universes, the beliefs and associated rituals [can] serve to dramatise aspects of the quest within (Heelas, P., 1996, p.89). In the words of Neville Drury, 'the shamanic technique opens up the possibility for each of us to discover our *own* inner mythology, to explore our own transpersonal archetypes, to find our own Dreamtime' (Drury, 1989, p.101). This can be regarded as representing a fair summary of how most neo-shamanic practitioners view what they do.

Whether such journeys are merely figments of the imagination or not is in a sense irrelevant as 'there is a ... strong empirical reason why we should hold beliefs that we know can never be proved. It is that they are known to be useful. Man positively needs general ideas and convictions that will give a meaning to his life and enable him to find his place in the universe ... It is the purpose and endeavour of religious symbols to give a meaning to the life of man' (Jung, C.G., 1977, p.247). Moreover, for the people involved in shamanism, 'Shamanic cultures have particular assumptions about what exists (ontology) and how things happen (causality). If one shares these assumptions, the possibility of effective shamanic action follows' (Vitebsky, P., 2001, p.143). For the 'insiders' it is as simple as that, and no further reasons are needed.

William James maintains that 'The good dispositions which a vision, or voice, or other apparent heavenly favour leave behind them are the only marks by which we may be sure that they are not possible deceptions of the tempter' (James, W., 1982, p.20). He then goes on to quote from the autobiography of Saint Teresa: '... a genuine heavenly vision yields to her a harvest of ineffable spiritual riches, and an admirable renewal of bodily strength. I alleged these reasons to those who so often accused my visions of being the work of the enemy of mankind and the sport of my imagination' (*Ibid.* p.21). The point being made here by James is that religious life can really only be judged by its results and that is the criterion to apply when analysing such practices. If this criterion is followed, the question of whether such experiences are merely figments of the imagination or not becomes irrelevant. The reality of the unseen cannot be proved. However, 'in the distinctively religious sphere of experience, many persons ... possess the objects of their belief, not in the forms of mere conceptions which their intellect accepts as true, but rather in the form of quasi-sensible realities directly apprehended' (*Ibid.* p.64).

> Unpicturable beings are realized, and realized with an intensity almost like that of an hallucination ... They are as convincing to those who have them as any direct sensible experiences can be, and they are, as a rule, much more convincing than results established by mere logic ever are (*Ibid.* p.72).

Some would consider the Sacred Teacher the shaman meets in non-ordinary reality to be nothing more than what is known as the Inner Voice. As Jung points out, 'our attitude towards the inner voice alternates between two extremes: it is regarded either as undiluted nonsense or as the voice of God. It does not seem to occur to any one that there might be something valuable in between' (Jung, C.G., 1959, p.132).

According to the Buryat version of the legend of the 'first shaman',

> Khara-Gyrgan, having declared that his power was boundless, God put him to the test. God took a girl's soul and shut it up in a bottle. To make sure that it would not escape, God put his finger into the neck of the bottle. The shaman flew through the sky, sitting on his drum,

discovered the girl's soul and, to set it free, changed into a spider and stung God in the face. God instantly pulled out his finger and the girl's soul escaped. Furious, God, curtailed Khara-Gyrgan's power, and after that the magical abilities of shamans markedly diminished (Eliade, 1964, p.68).

The Storyteller: Shaman and Healer

Like the shaman, the storyteller is a walker between the worlds, a mediator between our known world and that of the unknown – someone who communes with dragons and elves, with fairies and angels, with magical and mythical beasts, with gods and goddesses, heroes and demons, able to pass freely from this world into non-ordinary reality and to help us to experience those other realms for ourselves. He or she can show us how to confront our most deeply-ingrained fears, or teach us how to experience ecstasy or bring us face to face with death or terror of the spirit - with the infinite and incomprehensible. He is not only the archetypal magician but also the archetypal guide.

In many traditions storytelling is synonymous with song, chant, music, or epic poetry, especially in the bardic traditions. Stories may be chanted or sung, along with musical accompaniment on a certain instrument. For this reason those called folk musicians by foreign music enthusiasts could just as well be called storytellers. Their roles in fact are often as much spiritual teachers or healers, for which the stories and music are vehicles, as well as historians and tradition-bearers. In Central Asia, for example, the same Turkic term, *bakhshi*, may be used for both shamans and bards, and both may be called to their trade by spirits to undergo a difficult period of initiation. Indeed a bard can be described as a healer who uses music as a gateway to the world of the Spirit, and there is a magical dimension to reciting the epics. They use a fiddle or lute as accompaniment, and tales may run through several nights of exhaustive performance; one Kyrgyz bard is known to recite 300,000 verses of the *Manas*, the major Kyrgyz epic. For genuine initiates of these bardic disciplines, they draw directly on the conscious creative power of the Divine and transmit it through the words they speak and sing. This is not the same as

60

merely 'being creative' or 'feeling inspired', and involves considerable spiritual training.

The *dastan* [Turkic epic] is ornate oral history and an important part of the Turkic literature of Central Asia. Traditionally, dastans have been repositories of ethnic identity and history, and some constitute nearly complete value systems for the peoples they embrace. The primary, or "mother", dastans are those composed to commemorate specific liberation struggles. Set mostly in verse by an *ozan* [bard], more than 50 mother dastans are recited by Central Asians from the Eastern Altai to the Western Ural Mountains and as far south as Bend-e Turkestan in Afghanistan. Most dastans commemorate the struggles of different Turkic peoples against external aggressors, such as the Kalmuks and Chinese. (H.B. Paksoy,1987, pp.75-92).

In Turkey, the folk-poets of Anatolia are usually referred to as *ashiks*, meaning 'the ones in love' [with the Divine]. The ashiks, who belong to the Bektasi/Alevi faith, have wandered the plains of Anatolia since around the tenth century. They accompany themselves on the *saz*, a long-necked lute with three sets of strings, said to represent the fundamental trinity of the Muslim faith: Allah, Mohammed and Ali.

However, there is no need to travel so far afield in search of the storyteller as shaman. Ballads such as *Thomas Rhymer*, as closer analysis shows, are in fact shamanic journeys in themselves: There is clearly a great deal more to this ballad than first meets the eye because there is also a parallel with shamanic journeys into non-ordinary reality. It is the kiss that moves what Carlos Castaneda called the 'assemblage point' and initiates the process of the journey. As Castaneda explains through the teachings of Don Juan, what we call 'reason' is merely a by-product of the habitual position of the assemblage point. Dreaming (and/or visualization) gives us the fluidity to enter into other worlds and to perceive the inconceivable by making the assemblage point shift outside the human domain. The ballad is presented below, followed by more detailed analysis:

THOMAS THE RHYMER

True Thomas lay on Huntlie bank
A fairy he spied with his e'e
And there he saw a ladye bright
Come riding down by the Eildon Tree.

Her skirt was o' the grass- green silk
Her mantle o' the velvet fyne
At ilka tett of her horse's mane
Hung fifty silver bells and nine.

True Thomas, he pu'd off his cap
And louted low down on his knee
'Hail to thee, Mary, Queen of Heaven!
For thy peer on earth could never be.'

'Oh no, oh no, Thomas', she said
That name does not belang to me
I'm but the Queen o' fair Elfland
That am hither come to visit thee.

'Harp and carp, Thomas,' she said;
'Harp and carp along wi' me;
And if you dare to kiss my lips,
Sure of your bodie I will be'.

'Betide me weal, betide me woe,
That weird shall never daunten me'
Syne he has kiss'd her rosy lips
All underneath the Eildon Tree.

'Now, ye maun go wi' me,' she said,
'True Thomas, ye maun go wi' me;
And ye maun serve me seven years,
Thro' weal and woe, as may chance to be.'

She's mounted on her milk white- steed
She's ta'en true Thomas up behind;
And aye, whene'er her bridle rang,
The steed gaed swifter than the wind.

Oh they rade on, and further on
The steed gaed swifter than the wind;
Until they reach'd a desert wide,
And living land was left behind.

'Light down, light down now, true Thomas
And lean your head upon my knee;
Abide ye there a little space,
And I will show you ferlies three.

Oh, see ye not yon narrow road,
So thick beset wi' thorns and briers?
That is the Path of Righteousness
Though after it but few inquires.

'And see ye not braid, braid road,
That lie across that lily leven?
That is the Path of Wickedness,
Though some call it the Road to Heaven.

'And see ye not that bonnie road
That winds about the fernie brae?
That is the road to fair Elfland
Where thou and I this night maun gae.

But Thomas, ye sall haud your tongue
Whatever you may hear or see;
For speak ye word in Elflyn land,
Ye'll ne'er win back to your ain countrie.

O they rade on, and farther on,
And they waded rivers abune the knee;
And they saw neither sun nor moon,
But they heard the roaring of the sea.

It was mirk, mirk night, there was nae starlight,
They waded thro' red blude to the knee;
For a' the blude that's shed on earth
Rins through the springs o' that countrie.

Syne they came on to a garden green,
And she pu'ed an apple frae a tree:
'Take this for thy wages, true Thomas;
It will give the tongue that can never lee'.

'My tongue is my ain', True Thomas he said
A gudely gift you would gie to me!
I neither dought to buy or sell
At fair or tryst where I may be.

'I dought neither speak to prince or peer
Nor ask of grace from fair ladye!' -
Now haud thy peace, Thomas,' she said,
'For as I say, so must it be'

He has gotten a coat of the even cloth,
And a pair o' shoon of the velvet green
And till seven years were gane and past,
True Thomas on earth was never seen.
(Quiller-Couch, A. (ed),1910)

It is the kiss of the Queen of Fairyland that changes Thomas Rhymer's life forever, as the start of his descent into what can be regarded as the Lower World of the shaman is marked by that kiss. The Fairy Queen tells Thomas of the three paths that lie ahead and explains the meaning to him, acting as a guide or sacred teacher.

The first path is almost desert, flat, wide and straight as far as the eye can see. Although easy to journey on, it is of absolutely no consequence. It would appear to be a reference to an occupation that is easy and so leads to no rewards, expanding neither knowledge nor skill and devoid of any spiritual value. It offers a contrast to the traditional path of an initiate into shamanic practices, who often has to undergo great suffering and hardship along the way.

The second path is narrow, winding and treacherous with thorny hedges encroaching on both sides. Hazardous in the extreme, yet with a happy ending for it leads to the city of the kings. As we know, the king is always at the centre and in control. The suggestion is that after all the trials and tribulations of endangering oneself and surviving on a path upon which many obstacles are encountered, the reward for the righteous is entrance to the king, an honour indeed.

The third path is lush and green, meandering into forest and glade. It is a wild place where one could easily get lost. The Queen gives no explanation of this and quite simply says "This is the path to Fairy Land, and do not utter a word whilst in this land or you end up staying forever." This suggests that anything spoken in the otherworld is to be taken very seriously indeed.

The only material thing Thomas is given on his journey is an enchanted harp and it is used as a link between the two worlds. It can be regarded as the equivalent of the shaman's drum, the rhythmic beating of which was used to induce a trance state. In some cultures a musical bow was plucked in a rhythmic way to achieve the same state, and in others songs were sung. The Sufis use dance to produce the same effects. Other parallels can also be drawn between the ballad of

Thomas Rhymer and a shamanic journey but limitation of
space precludes further analysis here.

> A large number of myths and legends show the essential role
> played by a fairy, a nymph, or a semi-divine woman in the
> adventures of heroes; it is she who teaches them, helps them
> in their difficulties (which are often initiatory ordeals), and
> shows them how to gain possession of the symbol of
> immortality or long life (the miraculous herb, the magical
> apples, the fountain of youth, etc.). (Eliade, 1964, p.78).

In Thomas Rhymer the part is played by the Queen of Heaven.

According to Jung, the anima is the deposit of all
ancestral experiences of men with women. Consequently she is
archaic and likes to appear in Grecian or Egyptian garb, or as
Queen of Heaven (as she does in Thomas Rhymer), or even
Mother Church. In the process of introversion, the regression
of the libido back into the unconscious, the libido acquires the
treasure hard to attain, the numinous archetypes; and when it
progresses again into the outward world, it will be spiritually
transformed just as the hero is, who has been to the
underworld and returned safely to the land of the living. This
kind of controlled introversion was for Jung one of the most
important functions of religious rites and its parallel can be
found in this ballad.

Significantly, a link has been established by Peggy Ann
Wright at Lesley College in Cambridge, Massachusetts,
between heightened temporal lobe activity and shamanistic
experiences. These are soul journeys to distant realms of
experience in order to communicate with spirits, and to bring
back healing advice. Rhythmic drumming of the sort used in a
vast range of spiritual rituals excites the temporal lobes and
associated areas of the limbic system, as can the practice of
guided visualization. Moreover, each time a storyteller
introduces a tale starting 'once upon a time', he/she is inviting
the audience to transcend their linear concepts of time and

space and so enter a light state of trance. Consequently, as in the case of shamanic journeying and guided visualisation, storytelling can also be used to facilitate the development of what Danah Zohar calls Spiritual Intelligence – what we use to develop our longing and capacity for meaning, vision and value - and the power of storytelling is not to be underestimated. This will be examined in more detail in the final chapter.

Below is a contemporary German folktale adapted from the story *Bundles of Troubles, Bundles of Blessings* (Kronberg, R. and McKissack, P., 1990). This story parallels the shamanic journey to the Lower World and provides a good illustration of how storytelling can be used by the storyteller in the same way as journeying can be used by the shamanic practitioner - for healing purposes.

As Van Der Leeuw says,

> Occasionally life's power dwindles: it grows paler and loses its freshness; and all this must be prevented by a periodical turning over a new page in the book of life, so that it begins anew). ... In religious phraseology, ..."dirt" includes far more than mere filth. "Dirt" means all the hindrances and annoyances that prevent the perpetuation and renewal of life, so that some celebration must set the arrested current in motion again. The means employed, however, need not "cleanse" in our modern sense, provided only it is powerful.
> (Van Der Leeuw, G., 1938, pp.343-344)

This is not only what shamanic ritual can provide, but also what people hunger for, and what the healing power of the story can achieve.

According to Campbell, the four functions normally served by a properly operating mythology are 'to waken and maintain in the individual a sense of awe and gratitude in relation to the mystery dimension of the universe, ... to offer an image of the universe that will be in accord with the

67

knowledge of the time, ... to validate, support and imprint the norms of a given, specific moral order, that, namely, of the society in which the individual is to live, and ... to guide him ... through the whole foreseeable course of a useful life' (Campbell, J., 1973, pp.214-215). A good story can function as a teaching tool in just the same way – it can present the world in such a way that we no longer take it for granted, and it can provide a 'map' to help guide us through life.

Jurgen W. Kremer defines tales of power as 'those stories which reflect individuals' distinctive paths along the particular trajectories of their life histories. They are about the unfolding of the individuals' uniqueness' (in Doore, G. (Ed.), 1988, p.191).

> Tales of power are conscious verbal constructions around numinous experiences outside of everyday consensual reality, which guide individuals and help them to integrate the spiritual, mythical, or archetypal aspects of their internal and external experience in unique, meaningful, and fulfilling ways. ... The important thing is whether a shift in awareness is entailed. It is not the stimuli of the experiences that are crucial, but the nature of the experiences they induce. ... The experiences to be embodied in tales of power thus have to be of something that is felt as larger than the range of experiences controlled by the conscious purpose of wakeful, consensual consciousness (*Ibid.* p.192).

It seems to me that the following tale very much epitomizes what Kremer is referring to.

BUNDLES

> There once was a woman who had so many problems, so many worries, so many troubles... that at times she felt she had more troubles than anyone else in the world!

Well... there was one friend she knew who had quite a large share of troubles herself. But this friend seemed to be able to move through her troubles and come out the other side with her head still held high. The more the woman thought about her friend, the more she began to think "I could ask her to tell me how she deals with her problems and then I would know how to deal with mine."

The woman became convinced that this was the answer - so one day she knocked on her friend's door. The friend invited her in. They sat down and chatted together while they had a cup of tea. By and by the visitor told the friend why she had come to visit.

"Oh, but I can't tell you how to deal with your own problems" the friend told her, "only you know what are the right choices for yourself." The visitor's face looked so crestfallen that the friend added "But I could tell you some advice that someone once gave me that helped..."

"Oh would you? Could you?" the visitor encouraged her.

"Alright" the friend answered. "Why don't you let that part of yourself (gesture to self) that is connected to all that is (gesture to above and beyond) take over caring for your troubles."

"Well... alright."

It wasn't the kind of advice that she had expected. The visitor stayed a bit longer chatting, then she said goodbye to her friend and began walking home. On the way home she thought "I really have tried everything else I can think of - what have I got to lose?"

So that night, when everyone else was asleep, she shut her door, got into bed, sat there and said "That part of me (gesture to self) that is connected to all that is (gesture to above and beyond)... please - help me with my troubles. I don't know what else to do..."

Then she supposed she must be done, so she turned out her light, pulled up the covers and fell asleep... and that night she dreamed a dream... She found herself in a vast candlelit cavern, surrounded by grey bundles of all shapes and sizes, as far as she could see. Walking toward her was a woman

69

with flowing long white hair and dressed in a long dark cape.

"Who are you?" asked the dreamer "and what is this place?"

"This is the cave of the bundles of troubles and I'm the Keeper of the cave."

"Bundles of troubles?"

"Yes," the Keeper explained, "each person who walks the earth carries a bundle of trouble on their left shoulder." The dreamer turned to look and there was a grey bundle on her left shoulder - it had been there all this time and she never noticed! "If you wish," the keeper continued, "you can take your bundle down and exchange it for another."

"Really? Can I?" The woman lowered the bundle from her left shoulder. Oh it felt so good to put it down. Then she began picking up different bundles, feeling their weight, trying them on for size... She did this for hours until finally she said "Can I take this one? This one feels just right."

"Certainly" the Keeper said, "but first, why don't you open it up and look inside?"

So the woman put the bag down and pulled on the grey drawstrings and looked inside... "But these are the same troubles I brought in here!"The Keeper of the cave smiled softly and nodded. "That's usually what happens, but do not despair, for there is another bundle on your right shoulder that should help lighten your load."

The woman turned and saw another bundle on her right shoulder. It had been there all this time and she never noticed! Only this bundle was woven of silver and gold threads and it sparkled like a diamond in the sunlight. The Keeper spoke - "Why don't you take down that bundle, and look inside?" So the woman did. The bundle was light as down. She pulled the silver and gold strings and looked inside. And there were all of her experiences and all that she had learned. There were her talents, her gifts, her hopes and opportunities yet to come. The woman felt her heart fill with joy and she looked up to thank the keeper of the cave. But the Keeper of the cave was gone. All the grey bundles were gone. The cave was gone. And she found herself sitting up on her own bed with the morning sun streaming through the window, shining in her face.

'The frequency with which the spirit-type appears as an old man is about the same in fairytales as in dreams. The old man always appears when the hero is in a hopeless and desperate situation from which only profound reflection or a lucky idea – in other words, a spiritual function or an endopsychic automatism of some kind – can extricate him' (Jung, C.G., 1959, p.217-218).

> Often the old man in fairytales asks questions like who? Why? Whence? And whither? For the purposes of inducing self-reflection and mobilizing the moral forces, and more often still he gives the necessary magical talisman, the unexpected and improbable power to succeed, which is one of the peculiarities of the unified personality in good or bad alike. (*Ibid*. p.220).

In the case of *Bundles*, the spirit-type appears as a woman but the role she plays is just the same. Shape shifters have the ability to transform themselves (mentally or physically) into animals. A 'theriomorph' is a shape shifter, a being who can assume an animal as well as a human form. There are two types of shape shifting: changing your light body in the astral to power animal, and changing your physical form on the earth plane into an animal.

In myths and ancient pictographs, the shaman is often characterized by the distinctive ability to change himself from human into animal shape. Sometimes this change is a literal one, human flesh transformed into animal flesh or covered over by animal skin; in other accounts, the soul leaves the shaman's unconscious body to enter into the body of an animal, fish or bird.

71

It is not only shamans who have such powers according to tales from around the globe. Shape shifting is part of a mythic and story-telling tradition stretching back over thousands of years. The gods of various mythologies are credited with this ability, as are the heroes of the great epic sagas.

In Nordic myth, Odin could change his shape into any beast or bird; in Greek myth, Zeus often assumed animal shape in his relentless pursuit of young women. Cernunnos, the lord of animals in Celtic mythology, wore the shape of a stag, and also the shape of a man with a heavy rack of horns. In the *Odyssey*, Homer tells the tale of Proteus -- a famous soothsayer who would not give away his knowledge unless forced to do so. Menelaus came upon him while he slept, and held on to him tightly as he shape-shifted into a lion, a snake, a leopard, a bear, etc. Defeated, Proteus returned to his own shape and Menelaus won the answers to his questions.

Shape shifters can also be found in fairy tales. The transformed husband, wife or lover is a common theme. *Beauty and the Beast*, from 18th-century France, is probably the best known of the many 'animal bridegroom' stories to be found around the world.

Not all transformations are from human to animal shape. The Great Selkie of Sule Skerry, described in Scottish legends and ballads, is 'a man upon dry land, a *selkie* [seal] in the sea,' and he leaves a human maid pregnant with his child. Irish legends tell of men who marry seal or otter women, hiding their animal skins from them so that they cannot return to the water. Generally these women bear several sons, but pine away for their true home. If they manage to find the skin, they then return to the sea with barely a thought for the ones left behind.

Japanese fairy tales warn of the danger of *kitsune*, the fox-wife. The fox takes on the form of a beautiful woman in these stories, but to wed her brings madness and death. In

Tibet, a frog-husband is an unexpected source of joy to a shy young bride. He is not a man disguised as a frog but a frog disguised as a man. When his young wife burns his frog skin to keep her lover in the shape she prefers, the frog-husband loses his magical powers, gracefully resigning himself to ordinary human life instead.

In Native American legends, deer maidens are dangerous. In a Lakota version of the tale, a young man walking far from camp meets a beautiful woman alone in the woods. It is (he thinks) the very woman he has been courting, who has rejected him. On this occasion, however, she seems to be interested in him and looks even more beautiful than ever in her doe-skin robe. While they talk, he playfully threads the end of a rope through a hole in her robe - until a dog appears and barks at her. The young woman panics and turns to flee, returning to her own deer-shape, but the rope holds the deer maiden fast around her foreleg. "Let me go!" she cries. "If you let me go, I'll give you magical power." The man releases her warily, and the deer maiden disappears through the wood. He vomits profusely, sick with the knowledge that if he had made love to her he would have gone mad like other young men who had encountered the deer. After this, he lives alone, plagued by sudden fits of wild, deer-like behaviour. Yet the deer-woman keeps her promise and gives him this ability: his skill with horses is unsurpassed and also with other four-legged creatures.

Stories of shape-shifters let us journey into non-ordinary reality, at least in our imaginations, and they enable us to inhabit many skins. Above all, they serve to remind us that we are all living beings beneath the fur, the feathers, and the scales.

The Frog Sister-in-law, which was collected in the Republic of Georgia, not only involves a shape-shifting frog, but a shamanic journey to the land of the dead too. As a result of the wisdom learnt along the way, evil is defeated, and everyone lives happily ever after.

THE FROG SISTER-IN-LAW

There was a king who had three sons and the time came to marry them. The king said, "Shoot arrows with your bows, my sons, and wherever they land, take yourself wives from there". And so they did.

The eldest son shot an arrow, and it fell in the yard of a certain king. The eldest son married the daughter of that king.

The middle son shot an arrow and it fell in the yard of that same king's counsellor. The middle son married the daughter of the counsellor.

The youngest son shot an arrow and it fell into a swamp. The youngest son went, and with difficulty he found his arrow. He pulled it out of the swamp, and a frog jumped out after the arrow. The prince became angry. He hurled the frog away, but she came back to him. He drove her away and abused her, but she just would not give up and kept coming back to him. In fact, the frog followed him all the way back to the palace.

The king did not want to go against his word, and so he married his son to that frog. The older sisters-in-law laughed at their brother-in-law and rejoiced at his shame. The prince just kept quiet and put up with it all because he knew there was nothing else he could do.

The brothers went their separate ways and the youngest son remained with his frog. As soon as they were alone together, the frog removed her frog skin and turned herself into a beautiful young woman. She was such a beauty, so beautiful that the rays of her beauty lit up the whole house. She immediately set to work. She swept the floors, tidied everything up, cleaned, and put the dinner on to cook. Then she climbed back into her frog skin once again and a whole year passed like this, with the frog working as a housemaid.

The prince then called the woman-worker to him and said, "Let's settle our accounts. How much do I owe you for the year? I want to pay you for your work".

But the worker answered, "You don't owe me anything because I haven't been doing anything. I've spent the whole year doing nothing".

"Who, then, did all the work? Who looked after my house?"

"How should I know?"

So the young man decided to lie in wait to find out who was working in his house and he hid himself. The frog thought that he had gone away, so she took off her frog skin. She put it aside, and she became such a beauty that the rays of her beauty lit up the whole house. Then she began to bustle about. She cleaned everything up, mixed the dough, put the bread to rise and was in the process of lighting the kitchen stove. At this point her husband came out of his corner, grabbed the frog skin and threw it into the fire.

"Don't burn it or you'll be sorry!" she shouted. But it was too late.

From that day on the prince and the frog began to live together as husband and wife. Rumour of her beauty spread far and wide all over the land. The older sisters-in-law found out and were jealous.

Soon the king invited his sons and his daughters-in-law to him as guests. The frog sister-in-law sent a man to her older sisters-in-law: "I don't have enough paper for a dress, won't you send me a little piece?"

They answered, "We ourselves are sewing dresses of paper, and we don't have enough for ourselves". They believed their frog sister-in-law, so they really sewed themselves paper dresses in order to travel as guests to the king.

The frog sister-in-law again sent a man to her older sisters-in-law: "Won't you lend me your horse, your donkey or at least your dog, to ride to the king as a guest?"

"We ourselves need the horse, and the donkey and the dog". They dressed up in paper dresses and they sat: the eldest sister-in-law on a mare, and the second one on a donkey. Then they loaded their luggage on a dog and rode to their father-in-law.

75

But the frog sister-in-law said to her husband, "Ride to my native land and say: 'I ask you to send the red horse, the dark-blue horse and the white horse!'" Her husband did what she asked. On the red horse the beauty sat herself, on the dark-blue horse she sat her husband, on the white one she loaded their luggage, and they rode to the father-in-law.

When half of the journey remained, the frog sister-in-law cast a magic spell and rain pelted down. The older sisters-in-law, in their paper dresses, got soaked right through, and their dresses got soft and tore. They were too ashamed to enter the royal palace that way and to sit down at the table so they set off back home again. But the frog sister-in-law with her husband remained to be guests of the king.

The father-in-law very much liked his daughter-in-law, and he said to his son, "Let me have your wife". His son refused. His father said, "If, in one day, you plough and sow that field over there, then good; but if you don't, then I'll take your wife from you".

The son became miserable. You could not plough that field in a hundred days with six pairs of oxen, so how could he alone both plough and sow it in one day? He came to his wife. "What have you become miserable about?" asked his wife. Her husband told her about it. "Didn't I tell you not to burn the skin or you'd live to regret it! There's nothing we can do. Set out for my native land and say: 'I ask you to send the magic plough'. Take some seed with you too. The plough itself will plough and sow".

The prince did what she asked, but the king now required him to dig up and bring back all the grain that had been sown. "If you don't, I'll take your wife from you", said the king.

The prince came sadly again to his wife. She asked, "What have you become miserable about, my dear?" Her husband told her. His wife said, "Go to my native place and say: 'I ask you to send the magic black skein'. Throw it into the sown field. It will turn into ants, and those ants will gather the grain".

And so it turned out. The ants gathered all the grain, and they brought it to the king. The king counted up and said, "It's one grain short".

"But here they're bringing that too", said the prince. They looked, and sure enough, an ant was running towards them, shouting, "I'm bringing it, I'm bringing it!"

The king said, "By dawn, surround the whole castle with a stone wall. If you don't, I'll take your wife from you!" The prince went again to his wife and told her everything.

She said, "Go to my native place, and tell them to send me the magic mirror. They'll give it to you without any problem. Direct it at the castle, and a wall will appear around the castle". And so they did. In the morning everything was finished. The prince walked backwards and forwards along the wall, and he was very happy.

This time the king said, "If you succeed in bringing from your mother's little finger that ring which she took away to the other world, then good; but if you don't, then I'll take your wife from you!"

The prince went home sad. His wife asked, "What's wrong with you, my dearest?"

"My father ordered me to bring from the other world my mother's ring. And if I don't, he'll take you from me".

"Go to my native place", said his wife, "and say: 'I ask you to send the big shawl'. Throw the shawl over a tree and you'll find yourself in the other world".

And so the prince did. They gave him the shawl, he threw it over a high tree and he found himself in the other world. He saw an old peasant woman was heating an oven in such a way that sparks were flying, and she was leaning over it. The prince was surprised and asked, "Why are you standing over that stove?"

"Go on your way, and if you return, I'll tell you. Many people go there but nobody comes back".

The young man went further. He saw that an old peasant woman had heated an oven until it was red hot. She was bending over it, and she was tearing off her breasts and moulding them to the hot walls of the oven. "What are you doing, mother?"

"Go on your way, and if you return, I'll tell you. Many people pass this way, but nobody comes back".

The prince went further and he saw: a husband and wife had spread out a cow hide. They were lying down on it, but there was not enough room for them. "What's wrong with you? Why, on such a huge hide, can't you find enough room?" asked the prince.

"Go on your way, and if you return, I'll tell you. Many people go there, but nobody comes back".

The young man went further, and he saw a husband and wife lying comfortably on an axe handle. They were lying there, and it was a real pleasure to look at them. "How can you lie comfortably on a single axe-handle?" asked the prince.

"Go on your way, and if you return, I'll tell you. Many people pass this way, but nobody comes back".

The young man went further, and he saw a ploughman lying down with nine pairs of oxen and bullocks walking round him. They were rolling him, licking him, and slobbering all over him. "Get up, man", said the prince. "Why do you let these animals torment you?"

"Go on your way, and if you return, I'll tell you. Many people go there, but nobody comes back".

The prince went on further, and at last he reached his mother. "My son, what sort of misfortune has fallen on you that has compelled you to come here?"

"Father ordered me to come to you. If I don't bring him the ring from your little finger, he'll take my wife from me".

"Here you are, take it", said his mother, "and say this to him: 'The only thing I ever took from you, out of all your wealth, was this one little ring. But if you're pining for that too, then here you are! Take it, and take with it also the fire. Burn up in it'".

Her son took the ring, and returned. He went past the ploughman the oxen were licking, and the man said, "I was the head ploughman and unfair. When it was necessary to plough my field, I began to harness the oxen when it wasn't even daybreak, but still dark. And I unharnessed them again only at night. But when I was doing it for others, I harnessed them at midday and by dinnertime I'd already set them free. That's why I suffer like this".

He went past the husband and wife who were lying on the axe-handle, and they said to him, "We lived there in such good agreement too, and here we live like it as well".

He went past those who did not find enough room to lie on a cowhide, and they said, "There we couldn't get on at all either, and here we're tormented in the same way".

He went past the old peasant woman who was tearing off her breasts and baking them in the oven and she said, "When I used to bake bread, I didn't give anybody even a little piece; and here I am suffering for that".

He went past the other old peasant woman who was standing over the red hot oven and she said, "I didn't love my husband and was unfaithful to him, and this is how I'm suffering for it".

The prince threw the shawl across again and the other world became hidden. He came to the king and said, "Here's what your mother ordered me to tell you: 'The only thing I ever took from you, out of all your wealth, was this one little ring. So take it and the fire together with it; burn in it'".

He had only just said it when flames appeared and burnt the wicked king until nothing remained but his ashes.

Although stories of humans shape-shifting into werewolves are commonplace, those involving the fox are not so easy to find. The traditional Siberian tale that follows illustrates how dangerous it can be to judge people by appearances, as the wife of the one-eyed man discovers to her cost:

THE ONE-EYED MAN AND THE WOMEN-VIXEN

There once lived a one-eyed man who spent each night at home with his wife, but each day at dawn he left her and went off alone. His wife never knew why her husband did not come home by day, where he passed his time or what he did. So one morning she decided to followed him to the place where he spent his days.

When she got there she saw that he had changed his form: now even his one eye was gone and he was more ugly than ever. She was so disgusted by what she saw that she made up her mind to leave him for good.

The very next day she set out to seek her fortune and on her way she met a giant. The giant snatched her up and slung her over his shoulder, carrying her off to the top of a high mountain. Once there he flung her through the opening of a great *yurta*. Sore and scared, she began to weep. Her clothes were all torn and it was freezing cold. Now she bitterly regretted that she had deserted her husband because she thought him ugly. And when she thought of that, she cried all the more until suddenly she heard a voice.

'Come on, dry your tears. Look up and you'll see the skins of land birds hanging above you. Take them and put them on.'

The woman looked up and noticed a grass-braided basket hanging on the wall and in it she found a jacket made of crow skins. Taking the jacket she went to put it on but she could not because it was too small. Once more she burst into tears, and again she heard the voice whispering to her:

'Come now, don't cry. Look up and you'll find the skins of land animals; take them and put them on'.

Looking up she found some fox skins, so she took them down and tried to put them on. This time they fitted her well and soon she felt quite warm. Dressed in her new fox coat, she began to seek a way out of the yurta. Eventually she found it and set off on her journey home.

On the way, she felt thirsty and stopped at a stream to drink; but when she caught a reflection of herself in the clear water she was horrified to see that she had grown long fox's ears.

On she went and it was not long before she felt someone was behind her; as she turned her head she saw that it was her own fox's tail trailing her. Although she tried to shake free of the large red brush, she was unable to do so and had to proceed with the tail.

Shortly she arrived at the seashore where her father was just setting out to hunt seals. He was paddling along in his canoe when he saw the vixen standing on the shore, not seeming to fear him at all. Yet when he came up the beach and tried to seize her, she evaded his grasp and kept out of reach. He threw her some seal meat which she devoured greedily before running off into the trees. Only when darkness had fallen did she steal into her father's settlement towards his yurta. Over and over again she tried to enter his home, but each time she lowered her head to pass through the opening, her head itself seemed to jerk to the side and she was unable to enter.

In the end she made her way sadly to the fields and, there, people say, she remains to this day.

The **Lotus** (*Nelumbo nucifera*) is one of the world's most revered flowers. Its name is actually shared by a number of different plants with blossoms of various colours, but the most celebrated is probably the sacred white lotus of the Hindus. Its huge, almond-shaped petals form a shallow bowl around a seedpod that is vaguely reminiscent of the nozzle of a watering can. This magnificent blossom, rising on a tall stalk from a flat base of large, round leaves, is endowed with an exotic aura. In Buddhist tradition, lotus blossoms mark each of the seven steps in ten directions taken, paradoxically, by the newborn Buddha. But without a doubt it is the colour of the lotus, a blinding whiteness speaking of unblemished purity, that underlies its magical allure.

The lotus was an important icon in ancient Egypt, the inspiration for the Phoenician capitals that preceded the Ionic order of design, the sacred flower of Hindu religions and the object of the principal mantra of Tibetan Buddhism: *om mani padme hum*, which means "Hail, jewel in the lotus." Given the mechanical efficiency of prayer wheels that symbolically repeat those words without pause, the lotus may be the most frequently invoked plant in the world In various parts of the world it has been a symbol of fertility, birth, beauty, sunlight, transcendence, sexuality and the resurrection of the dead. But above all, the lotus represents purity.

The white lotus, born in the water and having grown in the water, rises beyond the water and remains unsoiled by the water. In the same way, the Buddha, born in the world, having grown up in the world, after having conquered the world, remained unsoiled by the world. Like the lotus that grows in muck but does not partake of it, the human heart should stay independent of evil thoughts in Buddhism's ideal. Guanyin, the Buddhist Goddess of Mercy alleviates humanity's sufferings by sprinkling drops of water as she walks over a bed of lotuses.

Fertility is the most important meaning that has been ascribed to the flower. According to Hindu mythology, after the great deluge the Almighty fertilized the waters to produce an egg. From one part of this egg came Brahma the Creator, and from another the universe. This is why the universe is called *brahmand* or the cosmic egg in Sanskrit. Another legend states that Brahma emerged from a lotus that grew out of Vishnu the Preserver's navel.

The flower's petals close to enable the plant to control its inner circulation of water, to avoid being affected by the weather. This phenomenon led the flower to acquire the metaphor for rebirth as it could seemingly transcend time. Some believe that the lotus came to India from Egypt. Later, Buddhism borrowed the flower from Hinduism. In Buddhist painting and sculpture, whenever Buddha is delivering an important sermon, he is shown sitting on a lotus pedestal. Buddhist scriptures enumerate fragrance, purity, delicateness and beauty as the attributes of lotus.

Indian literature abounds in references to the flower. Poets have compared a pretty face, dainty limbs and attractive eyes to the flower. The plant's steam is spoken of as the favourite meal of elephants. Its leaves have cooled the fires of many a noble lady separated from her beloved. And *kamshastra*

(The Art of Lovemaking) has four categories of women, the most beautiful and accomplished among them being the *padmini* or the lotus lady.

The flower is put to many uses. The thread taken from the leaf stalks is used for making wicks for oil lamps in temples and cloth made from this yarn is thought to cure many ailments. Besides, extract from the flower is used in both traditional and modern medicine. *Nelumbo nucifera* is a wholly edible species. Its seeds are roasted to make puffs called *makhanas* and the plant's rhizomes are a source of lotus meal, which is rich in starch. A number of wild animals feed on the plant and fish find refuge in its underwater stalks.

The blind man's daughter in the tale that follows is transformed into a Lotus. This *Shimchong* narrative was used in Korea in shamanic ceremonies and is evidence of the therapeutic power of storytelling. The "patient" was supposed to be healed precisely at the climax of the story when Old Man Shim opens his eyes and sees his long-lost daughter.

> In ancient medicine it was well known that the raising of the personal disease to a higher and more impersonal level had a curative effect. In ancient Egypt, for instance, when a man was bitten by a snake, the priest-physician was called in, and he took from the temple library the manuscript about the myth of Ra and his mother Isis, and recited it. Isis had made a poisonous worm and hidden it in the sand, and the god Ra had stepped on the serpent and was bitten by it, so that he suffered terrible pain and was threatened with death. Therefore the gods caused Isis to work a spell which drew the poison out of him. The idea was that the patient would be so impressed by this narrative that he would be cured. (Jung, C.G., 1977, pp.102-103).

If the patient is shown that his particular ailment is not only his problem but a general ailment – even a god's ailment – he is in the company of men and gods, and this knowledge can produce a healing effect.

83

The history of religion can be seen as 'a treasure house of archetypal forms from which the doctor can draw helpful parallels and enlightening comparisons for the purpose of calming and clarifying a consciousness that is all at sea' (Jung, C.G., 1968 2nd Edition, p.33). The message being conveyed is that if the figures we read about and identify with can overcome difficulties, then we can too.

Jung also made the observation that 'Suffering that is not understood is hard to bear, while on the other hand it is often astounding to see how much a person can endure when he understands the why and the wherefore. A philosophical or religious view of the world enables him to do this, and such views prove to be, at the very least, psychic methods of healing if not of salvation' (Jung, C.G., 1977, pp.698-699).

SHIMCHONG, THE BLIND MAN'S DAUGHTER

Long ago there lived a poor blind *yangban* by the name of Shim Hakkyu. He and his devoted wife, Kwakssi, were childless, and it was only after many years of faithful prayer to the spirits that Kwakssi bore a beautiful daughter. They called her Shimchong. However, the ordeal of giving birth at such an advanced age proved to be too much for Kwakssi, and unfortunately she passed away. Shim did his best to raise his daughter on his own.

Shimchong was an obedient and loving daughter who accompanied her father as soon as she could walk and begged alms with him the moment she could speak. It was not many years before she was a beautiful young girl. One day, Old Man Shim was out on his own and he stumbled into a deep irrigation ditch. As he was foundering about in the water, trying vainly to climb out and bemoaning his fate, he heard a voice speak to him from above. "Old man," it said, "I have heard you lamenting about your blindness. If you will give 300 bushels of rice to my temple as a tribute to the Lord Buddha, we will offer up our prayers to return your sight." Gentle but firm hands that seemed to reach down from the heavens themselves took hold of Old Man Shim's trembling arms and pulled him from the waters of the ditch. Shim was so thankful and so full of hope that he momentarily forgot his dire circumstances, and without thinking he blurted out, "Thank you kind monk. Thank you! Somehow I will give you those 300 bags of rice! I swear I will!"

It was only much later, when his elation had worn off, that Old Man Shim remembered he did not have the means to offer three bowls of rice - let alone 300 bushels - to the temple.

"How stupid I've been!" Old Man Shim said to his daughter that evening, recounting his misfortune. "What shall I do? I was filled with happiness and the world seemed a wonderful place to me. Other men jostle me out of the way or steal my alms from out of my hands but the monk was kind. All I wanted was to return his kindness, and look what I have done. What terrible thing will befall us if I have offended the Buddha himself?"

That night she lay on her thin bed mat unable to sleep, worrying about her father's promise to the monk. She could think of no way to raise the 300 bushels of rice, no matter how much she pondered it, and by and by she drifted off into a restless sleep. In her dreams, her mother appeared and told her how she might get the rice for her father. "Go to the harbour," she said. "There you will find a merchant looking for a young maiden. Go with him and he will provide the 300 bushels of rice."

It just so happened that the Dragon King of the East Sea was displeased with the merchant fleet and had sent foul weather and storms that had sunk ship after ship on its way to China. To appease the Dragon King, the merchants needed to sacrifice a beautiful maiden. So when Shimchong appeared and offered herself in exchange for the tribute for her father, the captain of the merchant fleet jumped at the chance.

The 300 bushels of rice were taken to the temple and the prayers to the compassionate Buddha were offered up as agreed, but Old Man Shim did not immediately regain his sight as he had hoped. The monks said that it would not simply happen overnight. Now Old Man Shim was not only poor and blind, but had lost his only daughter too.

The sea was calm at the beginning of the voyage, but soon the sky grew grey and ominous. The water, at first, was only choppy, but then it boiled as if the Dragon King himself were thrashing his massive body beneath the waves. Lightning flashed from the dark clouds and the wind ripped at the sails. The captain brought Shimchong out of the hold, dressed up in bright-colored bridal finery. Although Shimchong told him that she would leap into the waves of her own free will, he did not believe her, and he had her hands and feet securely bound. With the sailors all weeping for her, Shimchong said a quiet prayer and leapt overboard into the ocean. And just as she disappeared under the waves, the violent seas grew calm once again.

Shimchong descended into the cold water. As she sank deeper and deeper, the water around her was suddenly bright with light and she found that she could breathe. She looked around her in wonder as the minions of the Dragon King approached her, released her from her bonds, and escorted her to the magnificent underwater palace.

And Shimchong lived there happily, for it is said that the spirit of her mother also dwelt there. But after a time she grew homesick for the world of the surface, and she longed to see her dear father again. The Dragon King noticed how sad she was and called her to him. "I cannot bear to see your unhappiness any longer, Shimchong. I have seen how devoted you are to your father and it touches my heart, so as a reward I will send you back up into the world above." And with this the Dragon King transformed Shimchong into a lotus flower.

So it happened that a giant white lotus blossom was found at the mouth of a river along the coast, and the local fisherman, awed by its beauty, decided to make it a gift for their King. The King was recently widowed and they hoped the bright flower would lift his spirits.

When the King first beheld the flower, his eyes lit up in wonder. He rewarded the fishermen handsomely and had the lotus installed in its own special room where he would stand for hours each day in a melancholy mood, admiring its beauty. Each night Shimchong would emerge from the blossom, and at the crack of each dawn she would merge into it again. Time and seasons passed and the King's love for the flower did not wane.

One moonlit night the King was restless, and as he wandered the palace he found himself, by and by, at the chamber of the lotus flower. He stepped inside to gaze upon the lotus in the moonlight, but what he saw was far more wonderful—a woman so beautiful it took his breath away. "Who are you?" he said. "Are you a ghost come to bewitch me or are you real?"

"It is only me. My name is Shimchong and I live in the flower." Out of modesty, she tried to hide herself, but when she turned, she found the lotus flower had vanished.

And this is how Shimchong came to be the King's bride. There was a magnificent wedding, and they passed their days together in great happiness, but the King sensed a great sadness about his new Queen. One day he found her weeping in the garden. "My dear wife," he said, "I cannot bear to see your tears. Tell me your wish—any wish—and it shall be granted."

"There is only one thing I desire," Shimchong replied. "Let there be a great public banquet to celebrate our marriage, and let all the blind men of the Kingdom be invited to partake of the feast. That is what will make my heart glad."

The King honoured his Queen's strange request, and so from far and wide, from all corners of the kingdom, the blind beggar men were invited to a banquet to celebrate the wedding. For three days they came to drink and to dine on the fine foods, and each day the new Queen watched from behind her gauzy silk curtains, hoping that the next blind man might be her father. But it was to no avail.

On the last day, as the gates were closing and the Queen had turned forlornly away, a loud racket was heard outside. The servants were turning away a blind beggar who had arrived too late. And just as the gates were closing, the Queen happened to glance backwards to see that under the dirt and dust of his long journey and under the tatters of his rags, the old man was none other than her father. "Father!" she cried. "Father! It is my dear father! Let him in!"

Old Man Shim staggered inside, nearly losing his balance from the shock of hearing the familiar voice. "Aigo! Shimchong-ah!" he called. "Is it a ghost or have the dead come to life? My daughter! Is that your voice I hear? Let's have a look at you, girl!"

Once again, in his enthusiasm, Old Man Shim forgot his circumstances. He opened his eyes wide, oblivious to his own blindness, and when he did so he found that he could suddenly see. Before him was his daughter, more beautiful than he could have imagined. Shim wept with joy and embraced her, and she, too, was tearful with joy. Soon there was a happy commotion throughout the palace, and it is said that every blind man there who wanted to have a look at Shimchong, the devoted daughter, had his vision restored that day.

'A considerable number of initiatory motifs ... [can be found] in the literature that, from the twelfth century, grew up around the *Matiere de Bretagne*, especially in the romance giving a leading role to Arthur, the Fisher King, Percival, and other Heroes pursuing the Grail quest' (Eliade, 2003, pp.123-124). 'Most of these scenarios are initiatory; there is always a long eventful quest for marvellous objects, a quest which, among other things, implies the Heroes' entering the other world. ... The fact that people listened with delight to romantic tales in which initiatory clichés occurred to satiety proves, I think, that such adventures provided the answer to a profound need in medieval man' (*Ibid.* p.125).

> The majority of initiatory patterns when they had lost their ritual reality ... became ... literary motifs. ... They now deliver their spiritual message on a different plane of human experience, by addressing themselves directly to the imagination. Something similar had taken place, and long before, with fairy tales. [For example, what can be regarded

as a shamanic journey to the Upper World can be found in *Deutsche Marchen seit Grimm* – "The Princess in the Tree" – which was analyzed by Jung.] ... Initiatory scenarios - even camouflaged as they are in fairy tales - are the expression of a psychodrama that answers a deep need in every human being. Every man wants to experience certain perilous situations, to confront exceptional ordeals, to make his way into the Other World - and he experiences all this, on the level of his imaginative life, by hearing or reading fairy tales, or, on the level of his dream life, by dreaming (*Ibid*. p.126).

This is as true now as it was in the past, as can be seen from the books that become bestsellers in our own times, and also from the films that become the biggest Box Office 'hits'.

From tales of vampires through to *The Picture of Dorian Grey* by Oscar Wilde, it would seem that those who attempt to run away from Death frequently go on to regret it, and the following tale from Georgia offers no exception:

THE EARTH WILL TAKE ITS OWN

There lived a certain widow and she had an only son. The son grew up and saw that only he had nobody he could call father. "Why does everybody else have a father and only I don't have one?", he asked his mother.

"Your father died". "What does it mean *died*? Does it mean that he won't come back to us any more?"

"He won't come back to us but we'll all go there - to where he is", said his mother. "Nobody can run away from death".

The young man said, "I didn't ask anybody for life, but I'm already alive and I don't want to die. I'm going to find such a place where they don't die".

For a long time his mother begged him not to go, but her son did not listen, and he set out to look for such a place where they do not die. He went round the whole world. And wherever he went, he asked the same question, "Is there death here?"

"There is", they answered him.

The young man became sad: there is no such place where they do not die. On one occasion, when he was walking across a plain, he saw a deer with high branching antlers. The young man liked the deer's antlers very much, and he asked the deer, "Don't you know somewhere where they don't die?"

"There's no such place", said the deer, "but until my antlers grow up to the sky, I won't die; but when they grow up that high, my death will come too. If you like, stay with me and you won't die while I'm alive".

"No", said the young man, "either I want to live eternally, or I might just as well die where I come from".

The young man went on further. He crossed the plain, he went all through the valleys and reached the mountains. He saw a raven sitting on a crag, cleaning himself, and shedding his downy feathers into a huge deep gorge below. The young man asked the raven, "Don't you know a place where they don't die?"

"No", said the raven. "Here I'll live until all of this gorge is filled with my downy feathers, but when it's filled, then I'll die. Stay with me and live on until the time when I die".

The young man looked into the gorge and shook his head. "No", he said, "either I want to live eternally or I might just as well die where I come from".

The young man went on further. He passed through the whole world, and approached the sea. He walked along the shore, not knowing where to go. One day passed, two days passed, but nothing could be seen. On the third day he saw something shining in the distance. He walked towards it and there stood a crystal castle. The young man walked around the castle, but he could not find any kind of door. For a long time he was tormented, but at last he noticed a small streak, and he guessed that this was really the entrance. He pressed with all his strength and the door opened. The young man went inside and saw, lying there, a young woman of such beauty that the sun itself would envy her if it saw her.

The young man liked the woman a lot and she fancied him too. The young man asked, "Beautiful lady, I want to get away from death. Don't you know a place where they don't die?"

"There's no such place", said the young woman, "why waste your time looking for it? Stay here with me instead".

He said, "I wasn't looking for you, I'm looking for such a place where they don't die, otherwise I would have stayed there, where I have come from".

The young woman said, "The earth will take its own, you yourself would not want to be immortal. Come, tell me, how old am I?"

The young man looked at her: Her fresh cheeks, the colour of roses, were so beautiful that he completely forgot about death.

"Fifteen years old at the very most", he said.

"No", answered the young woman, "I was created on the first day of the beginning of the world. They call me Krasoy, and I will never become old and will never die. You would be able to stay with me forever, but you will not want to – the earth will call you". The young man swore that he would never leave her.

They began to live together. The years flew past, like a moment. Much changed on the earth. Many died. They turned into dust. Many were born. The earth changed its face, but the young man did not notice how the time had flown. The young woman was always just as beautiful, and he was always just as young. Thousands of years flew past.

The young man missed his old home, and he wanted to visit his people. He said, "I want to go and see my mother and family".

She said, "Even their bones no longer remain in the earth".

He said, "What are you talking about! Altogether I've only been here for three or four days. What could have happened to them?"

The young woman said, "As I've been telling you, the earth will take its own. All right, go then! But remember that whatever happens to you, you've only got yourself to blame". She gave him three apples and told him to eat them when he started to feel miserable.

The young man said goodbye to her and went. He walked, and he walked, and he saw the crag that the raven had been sitting on. The young man looked: all the gorge was filled up with his downy feathers, and there was the raven himself, lying all dried up. It grew dark in the young man's eyes, and he wanted to go back again, but already the earth would not allow him, it drew him forward. He went further, and he saw, standing on the plain, the deer. His antlers reached the sky, and the deer himself was dying. The young man realised that much time has passed since he left home. He went on further. He reached the area where he had been born, but he did not find either relatives or acquaintances. He asked people about his mother, but nobody had even heard of her. He walked alone and nobody knew him. At last he met a certain old man, and told him who he was looking for. The old man said, "That woman, as I heard from my grandfather and great-grandfather, lived once; but how could her son be alive now?" There went though the whole land the rumour about this person. But what they say about him! They regard him as some kind of freak.

The young man carried on walking alone. He came to that place where once there stood his home, and he found only ruins, which were already reddened with moss. The young man remembered his mother, his childhood, his companions, and he became sad. He decided to eat the apples that the young woman from the crystal castle had given him. He got out one apple, ate it, and suddenly there grew on his face a long grey beard. He ate the second apple, and his knees gave way, the small of his back bent and he fell to the ground without any strength. He was lying there, unable to move either an arm or a leg. He called a passing boy, "Come close to me, Boy. Get the apple out of my pocket and give it to me". The boy got the apple, and gave it to him. He took a bite of it and he died right then and there.

The entire village community came to bury him.

Folktales have been described as 'traditional tales, of no firmly established form, in which supernatural elements are subsidiary [the hero is always a human being]; they are not primarily concerned with 'serious' subjects or the reflection of deep problems and preoccupations; and their first appeal lies in their narrative interest' (Kirk, 1970, p.37). 'One special ingredient requires emphasis, and that is the use of trickery or ingenuity. Often the main point of a tale is precisely the ingenious way in which a difficulty or danger is overcome, or the solution to a problem or *impasse* is discovered. ... Folktales often exemplify, in addition, a kind of wish-fulfilment fantasy' *(Ibid.* p.38). 'Many folktales do not give particular names to their characters, but generic or typical names like "Jack the Giant-killer" ... This practice reflects at once the range of their appeal, their lack of specific reference and the importance of situation at the expense of character' *(Ibid.* p.39). 'The action of folktales ... is assumed to have taken place within historical time, in the past often enough, but not the distant or primeval past. Such tales are no more specific about period than about persons, but "once upon a time" implies historical time and not the epoch of creation, or of the first men, or of a golden age' *(Ibid.* p.40).

On the other hand,

> What are usually termed '**myths**' ... tend to behave differently. The characters, particularly the hero, are specific, and their family relationships are carefully noted; they are attached to a particular region, although the region may vary according to where the myth is being told. The action is complicated, and often broken up into loosely related episodes. It does not usually depend on disguises and tricks, but rather on the unpredictable reactions of individuals, personalities rather than types. Indeed one of the distinguishing characteristics of myths is their free-ranging and often paradoxical fantasy (Kirk, 1970, p.39).

> In myths the supernatural component often produces drastic and unexpected changes in the forward movement of the action. In addition, myths tend to possess that element of 'seriousness', in establishing and confirming rights and

institutions or exploring and reflecting problems or preoccupations, that has been mentioned although not so far discussed. Moreover, their main characters are often superhuman, gods or semi-divine heroes, or animals who turn into culture-heroes in the era of human and cultural creation. For myths, specific though they may be in their characters and local settings, are usually envisaged as taking place in a timeless past *(Ibid.* p.40).

Although this distinction between **folktales** and **myths** is clear enough, in practice it is often difficult to differentiate between the two forms as they tend to overlap – *The Earth will take its Own* being a good example of this.

The final story in this chapter once again involves shape-shifting. It comes from Tibet.

THE CASTLE IN THE LAKE

In the land of Tibet, there was a beautiful lake surrounded by hills and mountains. So beautiful and clear was the lake that people who passed by would gasp in amazement. Some would say that when the sun was high in the sky, casting the shadows of the mountain peaks across the calm expanse of water, it looked just as if there was a castle in the lake, a castle of such vast proportions that it filled the water. So the lake soon came to be known as "The Castle Lake."

Many stories grew up around the lake and its castle. Sometimes it was said that when the moon shone full and the stars gleamed like diamonds on the water, people could be seen rising from the lake, strange people, with eyes afire and flowing hair hanging like wet leaves around their faces. Or fiery dogs would appear to tear the flesh from lone travellers innocently walking along the beach.

But, as is often the case with legends, father told daughter and mother told son through many generations, until the stories grew bigger and bigger with each telling, and finally they conveyed much more than the original teller intended. Soon it was generally accepted that there was indeed a castle in the lake, and that the castle had a king. The king, it was said, had many retainers, men who by some misfortune or other had fallen into the lake, or who had been captured while walking alone on its shores and were forever after forced to remain in the service of the king.

One day a young herdsman was tending his yaks on the eastern side of the lake. Feeling a need for refreshment, he left his herd and made his way down to the water's edge. After he had splashed the cooling water onto his face, he lay back against a large rock, took his cheese and barley bread from his bag, lit a small fire to heat up his butter tea, and began to have his lunch.

While he was eating, Rinchen began to reflect upon his life. His mother was a cruel woman; she forced him to work hard so that she could buy new clothes and eat well, while he had to be content with a few cast-off rags and the scraps of food his mother did not want. Thinking about all these things, Rinchen began to cry. The tears rolled down his cheeks and sobs shook his body; he worked his fingers to the bone and yet his mother wanted more and more.

As the boy began to pack away his things he looked up and saw a man standing at the water's edge. The man was tall and dressed in a black *chuba* dripping with water, looking as if he had just come up out of the lake. Recalling the stories he had heard about the Castle Lake and the king's retainers, Rinchen began to panic, and was just starting to run away when the man spoke.

"Why are you crying?" The man asked. Rinchen turned to see the man and saw that his face was gentle and kind, and heard that his voice was soft and melodious. All the fear seemed to leave his body and he walked toward the tall man standing in the shallows of the lake. The man repeated his question so Rinchen told him about his mother and how she forced him to work harder and harder in order to keep her.

"Come with me into the lake," the man said, "because the king's a kind man and may be able to help you with your problem." The young herdsman began to feel fear welling up inside him once more because he was sure that if he went into the lake he would never return. The tall man sensed the

95

boy's fear, but in gentle tones which felt like music to the ear, he persuaded the young herdsman that there was nothing to feel anxious about.

"I'm one of the king's retainers," said the man. "I'll take you to see him and see that you return safely." The young herdsman thought for a moment, "What have I got to lose? My mother's so cruel that even death would be better than spending the rest of my life living the way that I do." And so, throwing his fear away, Rinchen followed the king's retainer into the lake.

The water was warm and friendly, and the boy was surprised that he could breathe quite freely. The king's retainer asked the boy to close his eyes as he led the boy through the water to the castle. When they stopped and Rinchen opened his eyes he saw that he was standing in a large hall, elaborately decorated in gold, shining silver, and beautiful shell. At the end of the hall was a throne, and on the throne sat an old man, the king.

The king beckoned to the boy to come forward and as he did so Rinchen noticed that he was not alone in the room with the king and his retainer. Standing on each side of the throne were more retainers, dressed in black *chuba*s just like the tall man who met him on the shore of the lake. When he reached the foot of the king's throne one of the retainers sprang forward and placed a small stool in front of the throne for the boy to sit on. Nervously, Rinchen sat down and looked up into the watery blue eyes of the king.

"Why do you come here?" asked the king in a deep voice which resembled the distant rumblings of thunder. The boy told the king his story, just as he had related it to the retainer on the shores of the lake.

The king listened, and when Rinchen had finished his story he turned towards his group of retainers and motioned for one of them to come to him. The retainer approached the king and bent low while the king whispered instructions into his ear. The young herdsman strained but could not hear what the king was saying. The retainer left the hall and returned a few moments later with a dog.

"Take this dog," said the king to the young herdsman, "but take care that you always feed it before you feed yourself, that's very important." Rinchen took the dog, and with his eyes closed let himself be led back to the shores of the lake. When he opened his eyes he was alone with the dog.

The young herdsman went home with the dog, and from that day on, whatever he wanted appeared before him. He would wake up in the morning and find that barley had been placed in the barley chest, butter in the butter chest and money in the money chest. Even new clothes appeared in his clothes chest. He was very happy and always took great care of the dog, following the king's instructions to always feed it before feeding himself.

Rinchen's mother was amazed that suddenly her son should become so wealthy, and one day she decided to go out with the herd of yaks to see if she could discover the source of infinite plenty. While the mother was out of the house the young herdsman decided to watch the dog, for he was curious and wanted to know how the animal managed to produce the money and food. Hiding himself in the house, he watched the dog as it entered the door, walked over to the hearth, and violently began shaking itself.

Suddenly, the dog's skin fell to the ground, revealing a beautiful woman, the most beautiful woman Rinchen had ever seen. The woman went to the barley chest, opened the lid, and placed in it the barley, which appeared from nowhere. Then she did the same with the butter chest, the tea chest, the money chest, going all about the house producing everything that the boy and his mother needed.

Rinchen could contain himself no longer. He seized the dog's skin and threw it into the fire. The beautiful woman begged him not to do so, but it was too late, the skin had burned quickly and was soon just a pile of ashes. Frightened that the chief's son would see the woman and take her for his wife, Rinchen covered her face with soot to hide her beauty, and kept her in the house away from the eyes of the people.

Soon, the young herdsman grew very rich, and with his wealth he grew exceedingly bold. "Why do I worry," he thought, "I've got so much money that the chief's son wouldn't dare to steal the woman from me because I can buy both weapons and men." Thinking this, Rinchen washed the soot from the beautiful woman's face and took her into town to show her to the people because he was very proud of her beauty.

The chief's son was in town and he saw the woman. He was determined that she should become his wife and sent his men to fetch the woman to him. The young herdsman was distressed and called upon the men of the town to help him, but they were too afraid of the chief and his son, and not one man would come forward to help Rinchen save his woman.

Feeling very sad, the young herdsman went down to the shore of the lake, sat down by the large rock and began to cry. Just as before, the king's retainer appeared. "Why are you crying this time?" he asked. "I've lost my woman," the boy replied, and told the whole story of how he had burned the dog skin and kept the beautiful woman hidden from the eyes of the people by covering her face in soot, but growing bold he had washed her face, showing her beauty to the chief's son, and so losing her forever.

The retainer asked Rinchen to follow him into the lake again because the king needed to be told the story. "Perhaps," said the retainer, "the king may be able to help you again." The young herdsman soon found himself in front of the throne once more at the feet of the king of the lake. After he heard the story of how Rinchen had lost the beautiful woman, the king gave him a small wooden box.

"Take this box," the king said, holding it out to the young herdsman. "Now," the king continued, "go to the top of a high hill and call the chief's son to war. When he's assembled his armies at the base of the hill, open the box and shout 'Fight!' " This the young herdsman did, and when he opened the box and called "Fight!" thousands of men charged out of the box and defeated the chief's son's soldiers.

Rinchen won back his beautiful woman and took her for his wife. He also took half of the chief's lands and became a rich, benevolent leader of the people. The young herdsman then returned the box to the king of the lake, thanking him for all his help, and he lived happily ever after.

The Lake features strongly in legends from our own lands too:

> Chretien de Troyes is a late reteller of the Arthurian legends in whose hands they have been converted into the familiar courtly romances. None the less, his version undoubtedly contains matter lost to us elsewhere. In his *Lancelot of the Lake*, the knight, in search of the abducted Guinevere, is directed to go to the sword-bridge – so named because it is like a sword laid edgewise – which no man has crossed. Riding to it we are told that Lancelot ceased to know "whether he was alive or dead" and even forgot his own name. After several days and many adventures he arrives at the bridge which flows over a river "as swift and raging, as black and turgid, as fierce and terrible as if it were the devil's stream." And he has not only the bridge itself to contend with, for he now sees that the far shore is guarded by two fierce lions. The lions of this story are plainly a surrogate for the dogs which occur in many other contexts, as for example in Altaic shamanism, and who, one must suppose, are related to Kerberus, the watchdog of Hades. Undaunted, Lancelot resolves to cross all the same and, before doing so, removes the armour from his feet and hands. Thus, unprotected, he passed over "with great pain and agony, being wounded in the hands, knees and feet". However, once on the other side he finds the lions were only figments of his own disturbed imagination. Here we have the Narrow Bridge in classically shamanistic form. In his deliberate use of bare hands we have a plain echo of the mutilations, often, self-inflicted, which the tyro shaman undergoes and, in some places, walking barefoot over upturned swords can actually figure in these. The fact that Lancelot is moving between the two worlds is made abundantly clear by the amnesia which afflicts him on his way to it. He is plainly in a trance-state. (Rutherford, 1986, pp.80-81).

As a conclusion to this chapter, the power of storytelling can perhaps best be illustrated with the following quote:

> In an empirically controlled experiment, Seligman reported that "merely telling a human subject about controllability duplicates the effects of actual controllability" (Seligman, M., 1975, p.48). In other words, a story which one is told, a narrative structure to which one is exposed (and Seligman is quite clear that it does not have to be "true" in the sense that it does not have to correspond to the actual state of affairs in the world of experience), can have the same effect as if it were a part of the world of real experience. By dint of imagination the human spirit can be seen to "escape history," to be "detached from the immediate reality." In other words, and to this degree, the human spirit is "autonomous" in that it is not wholly determined by its physical environment but contributes, through the imaginative generation of narrative, to the construction of its own determining environment. ... The point is that imaginative, narrative creations of the human mind, which can be enormously increased by a being of infinite creativity, themselves become a conditioning factor in human experience, and one which is historically revealed to be of the greatest significance. (Rennie, 1996, p.224).

Parallels between the Shaman and the Storyteller

The parallels between the shaman and the storyteller include the fact that they can both make use of a ritual framework, they can both produce the effect of the numinosum, and they both have the power to heal. The similarities and the differences will now be examined in more detail.

A basic ritual framework was explicated by Arnold van Gennep in 1909 - a tripartite model of **separation** (from everyday life), **testing** (the ritual proper), and **reintegration** (back into everyday life). The removal can be effected by such stimuli as music (including chanting and/or drumming), incense, candlelight or firelight, dressing differently or undressing, and the use of verbal formulae to set up sacred space. Cahill and Halpern also suggest there are three distinct stages in ceremony which need to be honoured for the experience to touch us deeply, and that these are the same psychological processes that compose our lives: **Severance**-leaving behind the everyday world, **entering Sacred Time & Space** - going beyond ourselves – leaving behind our limited identities and bringing forth a part of ourselves that we had not known existed, and **Reincorporation** - returning with new self-knowledge and a way to both integrate and use that knowledge in our daily lives. (Cahill, S. & Halpern, J., 1991) Effective storytellers and shamanic practitioners both make use of such a framework to achieve their desired outcomes.

In the case of storytelling, for example, severance occurs from the moment the storyteller says 'once upon a time'. The listeners go beyond themselves when they start to identify with the characters in the tale, and they return with new self-knowledge when they are able to draw lessons from the material presented.

'Sacred space may ... be defined as that locality that becomes a position by the effects of power repeating themselves there, or being repeated by man. It is the place of worship, independently of whether the position is only a house, or a temple, since domestic life too is a celebration constantly repeated in the regulated cycle of work, meals, washing etc.' (Van Der Leeuw, G., 1938, p.393). In view of the fact that the "etc." includes telling the people you live with about what happened to you during the day, the place where anecdotes and stories are told, possibly the living-room, also becomes a Sacred space, as does the stage or circle in which the storyteller performs. 'From time immemorial men have undertaken pilgrimages to places recognized as holy, where the Power of the Universe renewed itself daily, and where the heart of the world could be approached' (*Ibid.* p.401). Similarly, from time immemorial people have undertaken pilgrimages to places where stories are told, such as the village square, the stage of a theatre or a classroom in a school. Once again the parallel between the two can be seen.

> At a ceremony many of the conditions favourable to the calling forth of a religious thrill are given – the presence of truly religious people, acts and customs associated with religious feeling, a conscious detachment from the outer world, and, lastly, the important fact that an individual has been taught to expect a religious feeling at such times (Radin, P., 1957, p.11).

The same applies to any performance, a storytelling session for example, in that the audience has been conditioned to expect something special at such times too.

Jung refers to the archetype as 'an inherited tendency of the human mind to form representations of mythical motifs – representations that vary a great deal without losing their basic pattern' (Jung, C.G., 1977, p.228). 'One can perceive the specific energy of the archetypes when one experiences the peculiar feeling of numinosity that accompanies them – the fascination or spell that emanates from them' (*Ibid*. p.238). The archetype appears both in myths and on journeys and once again there can be seen to be a parallel between the two.

> A myth is an account of events which took place *in principio* , ... "in the beginning", in a primordial and non-temporal instant, a moment of **sacred time**. ... The myth continually re-actualises the Great Time, and in so doing raises the listener to a superhuman and supra-historical plane; which, among other things, enables him to approach a Reality that is inaccessible at the level of profane, individual existence. ... To transcend profane time and re-enter into mythical Great Time is equivalent to a revelation of ultimate reality – reality that is strictly metaphysical, and can be approached in no other way than through myths and symbols (Eliade, 1952, pp. 57-62).

Profane time can be transcended through both stories and by journeying.

> The essence of myth lies in its being told, in being repeatedly spoken anew. ... *It is the reiterated presentation of some event replete with power.* ... It arrests time, and in this it is sharply distinguished from celebration in the form of action, which utilizes the temporal instant, the *kairos*. Myth takes the event and sets it up on its own basis, in its own realm. Thus the event becomes 'eternal': it happens now and always, and operates as a type (Van Der Leeuw, G., 1938, pp.413-414).

In the same way, shamanic journeys are a means of arresting time, another characteristic they both have in common. Writing can be said to be a form of magic, 'one method of gaining power over the living word. ... According to Mosaic law, for instance, a woman suspected of infidelity had to drink water with which a curse, written on a piece of paper, had been washed off; thus she literally drank the curse, of course as an ordeal' (*Ibid.* pp.435-436).

It is written in the Old Testament that "Thou shalt not take the name of Javeh thy God in vain" (Exodus, 20: 7). The power that words are believed to hold is well illustrated by the way in which 'some of the Jews believed Jesus had learned the Mirific Word (true pronunciation of the name of God), and by the use of that fetish wrought his wonderful cures. In Jewish belief, this word stirred all the angels and ruled all creatures' (Maddox, J. L., 2003, p.216).

A '**wounded healer** is a shamanic term often used to describe a person who is called to the healing path. In traditional shamanic societies, the wounded healer experienced a near-death episode, a psychotic break, or a life-threatening illness. When someone has had an experience like this and returns to a normal life again, that person can understand the territories to be travelled in healing others. I believe that all of us who have made it to adulthood are in some sense wounded healers. We have experienced a variety of emotional and physical problems that allow us to have empathy for others who are suffering' (Ingermann, 1993, p.122). Without empathy, storytellers would clearly fail to reach their audiences in the same way as shamanic practitioners would be ineffective without empathy for their clients. Yet again it is evident that the two professions/vocations have a great deal in common with each other.

As Eliade points out, sleep deprivation

> is an initiatory ordeal that is documented more or less all over the world, even in comparatively highly developed religions. Not to sleep is not only to conquer physical fatigue, but is above all to show proof of will and spiritual strength; to remain awake is to be conscious, present in the world, responsible. [Dietary prohibitions or segregation and isolation can signify] death to the profane condition ... [and] transformation into a ghost, as well as the beginning of a new

life comparable to that of the infant. ... All these prohibitions – fasting, silence, darkness, complete suppression of sight or its restriction to the ground between the novice's feet – also constitute so many ascetic exercises (Eliade, 1958, pp.15-16).

Writers of stories have also been known to practise ascetic exercises in the hope of bringing about death to the profane condition and of finding inspiration. Examples that immediately spring to mind include William Burroughs and Aldous Huxley who both took drugs. So did Coleridge, who reputedly wrote *Kubla Khan* under the influence. Others went on the equivalent of vision quests, such as John Steinbeck who travelled around America in a truck named after Don Quixote's horse, *Rocinante*, and with a French poodle called *Charley*. The book that resulted from the journey was *Travels with Charley: In search of America*. Other writers, such as Paulo Coelho, have been on pilgrimages for the same purpose.

In the article by Jung in the book *Religion Today: A Reader*, religion is defined as 'a careful and scrupulous observation of what Rudolf Otto aptly termed numinosum - a dynamic agency or effect not caused by an arbitrary act of will. On the contrary, it seizes and controls the human subject, who is always rather its victim than its creator' (Jung in Mumm, S., 2002). A great many ritualistic performances are carried out for the sole purpose of producing at will the effect of the numinosum by means of certain devices of a magical nature, such as invocation, incantation, sacrifice, meditation and other yoga practices, self-inflicted tortures of various descriptions, and so forth. Those who listen to storytellers and those who undergo shamanic journeys both experience the effect of the numinosum. As Jung points out,

> We could have seen long ago from primitive societies what the loss of numinosity means: they lose their *raison d'etre*, the order of their social organizations, and then they dissolve

and decay ... Our spiritual leaders cannot be spared the blame for having been more interested in protecting their institutions than in understanding the mystery that symbols present ... We have stripped all things of their mystery and numinosity; nothing is holy any longer (Jung, C.G., 1977, p.254).

'Through repetition of the cosmogonic act, concrete time, in which the construction takes place, is projected into mythical time, in *illo tempore* where the foundation of the world occurred' (Eliade, M., 1965, p.20). This can be the case with both archaic rites and with stories.

'Profane temporal duration can be periodically arrested; for certain rituals have the power to interrupt it by periods of a sacred time that is non-historical (in the sense that it does not belong to the historical present)' (Eliade, 1957, p.71). 'The religious person can gain access to this alternative time through performance of ritual, narration of myth, and in "archaic" and "primitive" societies, by the performance of sacralized human functions, such as hunting, fishing, construction, and the more obvious sacraments (to the modern Westerner) of birth, marriage and death' (Rennie, B. S., 1996, p.80).

We have seen in the previous chapter that, for Van Der Leeuw '"Dirt" means all the hindrances and annoyances that prevent the perpetuation and renewal of life, so that some celebration must set the arrested current in motion again. The means employed, however, need not "cleanse" in our modern sense, provided only it is powerful' (Van Der Leeuw, G., 1938, pp.343-344). It is clear that this is what shamanic ritual can provide and what people hunger for, and that the healing power of the story can produce a similar effect.

Both listening to stories and shamanic journeying can provide a means of re-establishing contact with the sacred, so this is something else they both have in common. In the words of Eliade,

> In reciting or listening to a myth, one resumes contact with the sacred and with reality, and in so doing one transcends the profane condition, the "historical situation." In other words one goes beyond the temporal condition and the dull self-sufficiency which is the lot of every human being simply because every human being is "ignorant" – in the sense that he is identifying himself, and Reality, with his own particular situation (Eliade, 1991, p.59).

There are also clear **differences** between the shaman and the storyteller. According to Maddox, 'the social position of the medicine man ... depends upon the respect and fear which he is able to inspire by this attitude of aloofness and by the strength of personality, as well as upon the popular belief in his influence and power with the gods ... his power is thought to be without limit, extending to the raising of the dead and the control of the laws of nature' (Maddox, 2003, p.114). 'Among the Indians of Southern California, it is believed that the shaman can command the elements, read the future, and change himself into whatever form he wishes' (*Ibid*. p.115). 'Not only does the mystical influence of the shaman secure for him the respect of his people, but it also inspires them with fear of his dreaded person, of his ill will, and of his anger. Nansen says of the Eskimos, "By reason of their connexion with the supernatural world, the most esteemed angakoks have considerable authority over their countrymen, who are afraid of the evil results which may follow any act of disobedience"'(*Ibid*. p.119). These feelings that the medicine man/shaman inspires, referred to by Maddox, are clearly not the kind the storyteller is likely to engender.

In some regards the medicine man is a human parasite. He and his fellows make up a class which is non-productive of material goods. Their necessities and even luxuries are provided by those who toil. Their non-participation in the competition for life, their superabundance of leisure time, and the wide range of pleasure available to them are made possible at the expense of "the forgotten man" (Maddox, J. L., 2003, p.127).

In this respect the shaman is perhaps similar to the professional storyteller. However, 'without a leisure class it would seem impossible among savage as well as among civilized peoples for any intellectual progress or culture to be attained' (*Ibid.* p.128). Moreover,

> since the medicine men are the preservers of the legends and traditions of the tribe, and of the art of writing, they either actively or passively become teachers of tribal lore and wisdom to the younger generation. In Mexico, in Oceania, and in Central California, the shamans gave long and careful instruction, physical, mental, and moral, to the boys and young men of their respective peoples (Ibid. p.129).

The way in which both the shaman and the storyteller can be regarded as healers is worth highlighting too: 'When man falls ill, whoever cures him is his saviour, and thus healing pertains to the operations of salvation in its most essential sense. ...Today too the soul's salvation still demands the cure of the body just as, conversely, every successful physician is regarded as one who, in a sense, bestows salvation. The Christian churches, however, have to some degree forgotten this connection, and are consequently penalized by the success of so many movements and prophets, like 'Christian Science', that achieve faith cures. For man realizes that, despite all artificial isolation, conversion and healing go together, as will become still clearer with reference to holy men'.(Van Der Leeuw, G. 1938, p.109).

An example of the way in which the storyteller, adapting shamanic techniques, can act as a healer can be found in Michael Harner's book:

> A current example of a mutually supportive combination of shamanism with Western technological medicine is the well-known work of Dr. O. Carl Simonton and Stephanie Matthews-Simonton in treating cancer patients. … As part of their treatment, patients relax in a quiet room and visualize themselves on a walking journey until they meet an "inner guide," which is a person or an animal. The patient then asks the "guide" for help in getting well. This resemblance to the shamanic journey, the recovery of a power animal, and its shamanic use is as obvious as it is remarkable. … The Simontons found that they could train their patients to visualize the sending of their white blood cells to ingest the cancerous cells and expel them from the body much as a shaman visualizes and commands his spirit helpers to suck up and remove harmful power intrusions from the body of his patient (Harner, M., 1990 Third Edition, p.137).

The Simontons make use of guided visualisation – directed rather than free 'journeying' – which takes the form of a story. Examples of scripts for guided visualisation can be found in the final chapter of this book.

According to Alan Maley, 'we use stories as a way of making sense of the world. We use narrative as a way of integrating our experiences into our present understanding'. There follows a personal narrative of a young boy, taken from Maley's article, in which 'we can feel him struggling to make sense of his father's recent death. The mix of past and present tenses, the fractured punctuation, the switching of time zones, the blend of fact and fantasy ~ all point to his confused struggle to make sense of his recent experience. And that is what we all do to a degree'.

My father is on the broad side and tall side. My father was a
hard working man and he had a lot of money. He was not fat
or thin… His age was about 30 years when he died, he had a
good reputation, he is a married man. When he was in
hospital I went to see him every Sunday afternoon. I asked
him how he was going on, he told me he was getting a lot
better. My father was very kind to me and gave me and my
cousins cigarette cards. He likes doing woodwork, my father,
for me, and he likes a little game of cards now and then; or a
game of darts. He chops wood and saws the planks and he is
a handsome man but he is dead. He worked in the rubber
works before he died. (Maley,A. , Sept.2004)

Shamanic practitioners, when they recount the
experiences they have on their 'journeys' to their clients and/or
audiences, are doing exactly the same thing as the boy was
trying to do when he wrote the above story. In other words,
they are trying to **make sense of the world** they live in, trying
to gain a deeper understanding of this reality from what they
discover on their journeys into non-ordinary reality. It can be
seen from this that being a shaman also means being a
storyteller and the two go hand-in-hand.

Finally, the shamanic séance and the telling of a story
can both be regarded as **performances**, yet another feature they
both share in common. 'Performance – whether religious,
artistic, or sporting – is something done in front of other
people, the ones who as observers ultimately give it meaning.
This is the case with traditional shamanism [and also the case
with storytelling] (Stone, A., 2003, p.123). Stone goes on to add
the interesting observation that 'this is where many forms of
neo-shamanism part company most significantly from the
traditional shamanisms of Eurasia and America. They are so
often presented as solitary pursuits that are primarily of
importance to the practitioner as an individual or to a small
group of fellow practitioners' (*Ibid*. p.123).

There is [also] a degree of similarity between actor and shaman. Both engage in transforming themselves into something or someone else. And while performing each exists in a place that is simultaneously in this world and somewhere beyond it. [The same applies to the storyteller]. But while they are immersed in their make-believe world actors do not do the things that a shaman does. Likewise, the theatre audience might suspend disbelief but they do not actually believe that what is happening on stage is real [whereas shamanists attending a séance do] (*Ibid*. p.91).

'Being a shaman is ultimately a public role and the shaman's inner experience reaches its culmination and its full significance only as part of public performance. To say that shamanic action is sometimes highly theatrical is not to imply that the shaman is "only acting", as though this were something false. Rather, the performance transforms the inner reality or consciousness of a whole range of people who are involved in a number of different ways' (Vitebsky, P., 2001, p.120). Being a storyteller is ultimately a public role too and professional storytellers are constantly judged for their effectiveness in the same way as shamans are. It is interesting to note that

In Siberia, some shamans suffer if they have not performed for a long time. Recently among the Evenk a female shaman fell ill and asked another herdswoman to heat a piece of iron until it was red hot and then give it to her. She took it and began to lick it and the iron hissed until it became cold. The shaman said that her soul felt at ease at last, she fell into a deep sleep and awoke the next morning fit and healthy again (*Ibid* p.123).

It is highly likely that out-of-work storytellers suffer if they have not performed for a long time too – not only in a psychic sense but also financially!

111

The Use of Ritual in Storytelling

By itself, ritual creates change. In order to use ritual, one's body, mind, and spirit must get involved. The mind develops the ritual, the body actually performs it, and the spirit acts as a guide and witness at the ritual. This process alerts our psyche that a change is about to occur. So much of our energy goes into preparing and performing the ritual that the psyche takes this act very seriously and follows up by making the appropriate change. ... Doing any ritual with a group raises the power of the intention. A group also provides witnesses to what has been done, which heightens the level of commitment for the participants, and it allows community support (Ingermann, S., 1993, pp.88-89).

'Ritual loses its power and meaning if it is simply followed like a recipe. It must come from your heart. ... The way you come to the ritual is what creates the power – the intention and commitment, not the form' *(Ibid.* pp.93-94). 'We can use ritual or ceremony as a way to release any limiting beliefs or attitudes we are holding onto that block us from using our creative potential' *(Ibid.* p.102).

Ritual can be used in a storytelling session just as it can be used by the shaman in a séance, and the material presented in the chapter will illustrate this, The focus will be on stories and rituals related to Fire and Water.

FIRE

Fire, which produces heat and light, results from the rapid combination of oxygen, or in some cases gaseous chlorine, with other materials. The light is in the form of a flame, which consists of glowing particles of the burning material and certain gaseous products that are luminous at the temperature of the burning material. The conditions necessary for the existence of fire are the presence of a combustible substance, a temperature high enough to cause combustion and the presence of enough oxygen or chlorine to enable rapid combustion to continue.

Fire has been produced by two principal methods, friction and percussion. In the friction method, friction raises the temperature of a combustible material (kindling) to ignition temperature. The percussion method produces a spark to set kindling afire. In some cultures people have used and still use chiefly the friction method, in which two pieces of wood surrounded by combustible material are rubbed together until the ignition temperature is reached. In the stick-and-groove method, a stick is rubbed in a groove in another piece of wood. In the fire-drill method, a stick is rotated rapidly in a pit in a stationary piece of wood. The stick is rotated by rubbing it between the palms of the hands or by moving back and forth a wooden bow whose string is wrapped around the stick. The most basic percussion method of producing fire is striking together two pieces of flint, or by striking flint against pyrite or steel. The flint-and-steel method prevailed throughout the civilized world until about 1827, when matches came into use. With matches, friction is used to heat the tip of the match to the point at which chemicals in the match head ignite.

The use of fire probably developed in four stages. First, people observed about them natural sources of fire, such as volcanoes and trees set afire by lightning. Second, they acquired fire from natural sources and used it for warmth, light, and protection from predators. Third, they learned to make fire whenever they chose. Finally, they learned to control fire for use in smelting metal ore, in baking pottery, and in numerous other ways to help create new technologies and make life more comfortable. The keeping and use of fire probably had an influence in ending nomadic lifestyles and consequently influenced the development of the social and political institutions connected with members of a society having a permanent home.

As for shamans, they 'are held to be "masters over fire" – for example, they swallow burning coals, touch red-hot iron, walk on fire' (Eliade, M., 1958, pp.85-86). 'Access to sacrality is manifested, among other things, by a prodigious increase in heat' (*Ibid.* p.86). In Japan, for example, 'By enduring cold the shaman ... is able to activate in himself that magical heat which with the shaman in so many parts of the world is the proof that he has risen above the ordinary human condition. By demonstrating that he is in the grip of this interior heat, the shaman shows that he is possessed of power, particularly of that power which Eliade singles out as distinctively shamanic in character, mastery of fire' (Blacker, C., 1999, p.93) Interestingly, this does not seem to feature to any great extent in neo-shamanism, where practitioners do not appear to be prepared to go to such extremes. Today people want thing easy and such ascetic practices are no longer in vogue.

The story that follows makes us look with new eyes at what we take for granted.

RABBI JOSHUA AND THE EMPEROR OF ROME

The Emperor of Rome once said to Rabbi Joshua, "If you have a God, show Him to me. Then I'll know that He's real." Rabbi Joshua said, "Then come with me and I'll show you." And they went out into the street. Rabbi Joshua told the Emperor to look up at the sky, but the emperor could not because the sun was shining so brightly. So Rabbi Joshua said, "The sun is just a servant of God, and you are unable to look at it. Then how do you expect to see God Himself?" The emperor was embarrassed and went home.

Of the many different Creation Myths that attempt to explain the origin of Light, the following Alaskan Inuit tale is perhaps one of the most striking with its almost surreal imagery:

THE FEATHER BABY

In the early times, there was only darkness; there was no light at all. At the edge of the sea a woman lived with her father. One time she went out to get some water. As she was scraping the snow, she saw a feather floating toward her. She opened her mouth and the feather floated in and she swallowed it. From that time she was pregnant.

Then she had a baby. Its mouth was a raven's bill. The woman tried hard to find toys for her child. In her father's house was hanging a bladder that was blown up. This belonged to the woman's father. Now the baby, whose name was Tulugaak (Raven), pointed at it and cried for it. The woman did not wish to give it to him but he cried and cried. At last she gave in and took the bladder down from the wall and let the baby play with it. But in playing with it, he broke it. Immediately, it began to get light. Now there was light in the world, and darkness, too.

When the woman's father came home, he scolded his daughter for taking the bladder down from the wall and giving it to the child. And when it was light, Tulugaak had disappeared.

The Element of Fire was supposedly unknown to the earliest people. However, rather than being given fire by the gods, most primitive peoples say they had to steal it. According to the origin myth of the Amahuaca of eastern Peru, fire was stolen from the stingy ogre, Yowashiko, by a parrot who flew away with a burning brand in its beak. Angered by the theft, Yowashiko tried to douse the flames by sending rain. However, other larger birds spread their wings over the parrot to keep the flames alive so that eventually fire became available to everyone. This account has a parallel in Greek mythology, in which Prometheus stole fire from the gods and gave it to mankind.

Origin myths often tell of a rudimentary earth with many shortcomings and imperfections that, one by one, had to be removed or overcome. One belief is that at first, night did not exist and there was only day. The sun stood at zenith all the time and its rays beat down unmercifully on the ancestors. Sleep was all but impossible, and people lacked the privacy that only darkness can afford. Some tribes say night did exist but it was the hidden possession of some mythical being, and before everyone could reap its benefits, night had to be found and released. The Tenetehara of eastern Brazil, for instance, say that night belonged to an old woman who lived deep in the forest and who kept it enclosed in several clay pots. It was finally wrested from her and given to the tribe by a native hero named Mokwani.

The Kamayura of central Brazil and many other tribes have the opposite belief. They hold that in the beginning there was only night. It was so dark, in fact, that people could not see to hunt or fish or plant, and so were slowly starving to death. Then they discovered that the birds owned day and decided to get it from them. Ultimately, they were successful, and day was sent to the Kamayura decked in the brilliant plumage of the red macaw. The American Indian origin myth that follows presents a variation on this theme. The Coyote is the equivalent of the Trickster archetype. The countless tales in which he features are especially popular with the young. This can be explained by the fact that they teach through humour. The American Indians say humour is sacred and it is often the most effective means of getting your message across. The Yellow Jackets featured in the tale seem to be wasps or bees:

HOW COYOTE BROUGHT FIRE

Long ago, the animal people had no fire. They huddled together in their houses in the dark, and ate their food uncooked. In the winter, they were so cold that icicles hung from their fur and they felt very sorry for themselves.

Then one day, Wise Old Coyote gathered everybody together. "We have heard about fire," he said. "But the only fire is far upriver, at the world's end. It's guarded by the Yellow Jacket sisters on top a snowy mountain. They are wicked, and will not share it. But listen, if we all cooperate and work together, I am sure we can steal the fire" There was much fearful murmuring about the Yellow Jacket sisters, but all grew quiet as coyote told them his plan. Then he went on his way.

Grandfather Coyote slowly trudged up the mountain at the world's end. When at last he came to the Yellow Jacket's house, smoke was rising from the chimney. Coyote looked inside. The three old sisters were sitting around the fire. Coyote said, as friendly as can be, "If you let me in, I'll make you all look pretty." Suspicious, the three sisters put their heads close together and buzzed. "Come in," they said. "But no tricks!"

Old Man Coyote sat down and took a chunk of oak bark between his toes and held it in the fire. When it had burned into a blackened coal, he marked their yellow faces and bodies with black stripes to make them pretty. "Now," said Coyote, "if you close your eyes, I will make you even prettier."

Here was Coyote's chance! While the Yellow Jackets' eyes were closed, he took the charred oak in his teeth, and as silent as the moon in the sky, he crept outside. Then he raced down the mountain like the wind. When the Yellow Jacket sisters found out that Coyote had tricked them, they were absolutely furious. They too, flew like the wind. And it wasn't long until they caught up to Coyote. They were almost on him when Coyote tripped, rolled downhill like a snowball, and landed with a bump at Eagle's feet.

Snatching the glowing coal in his talons, Eagle spread his wings and took to the sky. Eagle was swift, but the Yellow Jackets soon caught up with him. Suddenly, Eagle dropped the coal. Below, Mountain Lion caught it in his great teeth

117

and bounded off through the snow. But still, the furious Yellow Jackets followed.

Just as they were about to sting Mountain Lion, Fox snatched the fiery coal, and escaped into the cover of the forest. Fox ran and ran, until she was so tired, she couldn't take another step. She huffed and huffed. Her breath made clouds, and the Yellow Jackets were right behind her.

Just in time, Bear took the fire and made his getaway through some sharp brambles. Bear, too, was quick, yet the Yellow Jackets were right on top of him. Even Bear could not fight them off, and he finally collapsed in exhaustion. As Bear fell, Measuring Worm, the Long One, took the fire. The Long One stretched way out over three ridges, yet still the Yellow Jackets were there, waiting, ready to strike.

Somehow, right under the Yellow Jacket's eyes, Turtle sneaked in, grabbed the fire, and scrambled off. But of course Turtle was slow, and one of the Yellow Jacket sisters stung him in his tail, Akee! Akee! Akee! Turtle pulled in his head and legs and flip-flopped down the hill. Fallumph! Fallumph.!Fallumph.!

The Yellow Jackets were swarming all over Turtle, when Frog leaped out of the river and swallowed the fire. Gulp! Then Frog hopped back into the river - plop - and sat on the bottom. The Yellow Jackets stormed the river, circling once, circling twice, circling three times, buzzing angrily over the surface. They waited and they waited and they waited, but Frog held the fire, and his breath. Finally the Yellow Jackets gave up, and flew back home.

As soon as the Yellow Jacket sisters were gone, Frog burst out of the water, and spat the hot coal into the root of a willow growing alongside the river. The tree swallowed the fire, and the animal people didn't know what to do. Then once again Coyote came along, and the animal people said, "Grandfather, you must show us how to get the fire from the willow." So Old Man Coyote, who is very wise and knows these things, said, "Hah" and he showed them how to rub two willow stick together over dry moss to make fire.

From that time on the people have known how to coax fire from the wood in order to keep warm and to cook their food. And at night in the season of the cold, they have sat in a circle around their fires and listened as the elders told the old stories. And so it is, even to this day.

In the world of shamanism, all the Elements have their source in the spirit world, which can be contacted for any number of purposes. Fire and heat are traditionally associated with ecstatic journeys. Shamans the world over use intense heat to purify themselves prior to ceremonies and rituals. These heat purifications were probably the early origins of the sauna and the Turkish Bath. The American Indian practice of the sweatlodge is an example of such a process that continues to this day. The steam produced by pouring water on the white hot rocks in the fire pit is used for the cleansing and revivifying of body, mind and spirit. When used ceremonially, smoke and heat from a fire can be used to carry the shaman up to the sky realm and to the land of the spirit. This is the basic significance behind the American Indian use of the pipe. When the pipe is lit and shared, all present are united through the world of spirit. In Scandinavia the bodies of Viking chiefs were cremated in longships, the rising smoke representing a return of the spirit to the sun, the giver of life. Communication with the Elements teaches us to become more fully integrated with the powers that surround us. We are then part of nature, not an antagonist or victim of it.

In the Imbas Forosna ceremony, the Druids entered a sensory-depravation chamber like those monastic beehive huts that dot the west coast of Ireland. The Druid would remain under a pile of skins with other Druids standing above chanting, perhaps for days, until finally the Druid is thrown out of the hut by surprise. They thought that the shock of being thrust from deep darkness into bright outdoor light would push the mind into a higher state of consciousness.

There is no need, however, for Fire Ceremonies to be elaborate. You can write your prayers or desires on a small slip of paper, pronounce the words aloud, sign the statement, and then burn it. If any bit of the paper remains legible after the embers cease to burn, it can then be used as a focus for meditation. Perhaps what remains on the paper holds a teaching for you.

We are largely made up of water, we breathe air, we produce heat and we depend on the earth for food so all of the essential elements are represented inside us. Yet we imagine we are somehow separate and different from what appears to be outside of us. Moreover, for those of us living in big cities where we are shielded from the effects of the Elements, this sense of separation becomes even more apparent. This is why working with the powers of Nature can be so beneficial for people like us.

According to Greek Mythology, when man was first created he was defenceless and had to huddle in the dark because all valuable gifts were used up on the animals that had been created before him. Prometheus was a Titan who took pity on mankind, stole fire from Mount Olympus, and gave it to man to protect him and light his nights. Prometheus also taught mankind how to harness the wind, tame animals, raise crops, and how to build houses. But he didn't stop there - he also taught man the basic sciences and how to use technology to be master of his world. This was an unforgivable offence to the other gods. Zeus punished Prometheus by having him chained to a mountain. An eagle was sent to tear out his liver every day and eat it, at night his liver would grow back. Prometheus was eventually freed by the demigod Hercules. He symbolises the courage needed to challenge the decree of the gods and unyielding strength that resists oppression.

Imagine now that what follows is being spoken by your **guide** in a gentle trance-inducing voice, as you embark on a guided visualisation to the Prometheus within you.

Make yourself comfortable and close your eyes. Take a few deep breaths to help you relax. Breathe in the light and breathe out all your tightness. Feel the tension disappear stage by stage from the top of your head to the tips of your toes. Let your surroundings fade away as you gradually sink backwards through time and actuality and pass through the gateway of reality into the dreamtime

Sometimes it feels as if everything and everyone is conspiring against you and you have no control over your life. It makes you feel like giving up. You find yourself facing a mountain and there seems no way of reaching your goal. But you turn now to your inner voice for guidance and a back entrance to the mountain is revealed to you.

You stoop down low to enter the mouth of the cave. You step out of the sunlight and into the darkness. Inside, once you grow accustomed to your new surroundings, you find a flight of steps, carved out of the rocks, leading up to an opening in the roof high above you. With each step you take, climbing higher and higher, you find your resolve mounting too, your determination to become your own master once more. And as you climb higher, the daylight that shines through the opening grows stronger, and finally you step out on to the summit. There you find Prometheus in all his glory waiting for you. Take a minute of clock time, equal to all the time you need, to introduce yourself and to put into words what you're looking for .....

If you're expecting sympathy, forget it because Prometheus has no pity for your plight. But he knows that by making this journey you've resolved to bring about change and he is willing and ready to help you. Take a minute of clock time, equal to all the time you need, to look within, to see how you've failed to honour your birthright by not taking control of your destiny .....

"I've been waiting for you but you can expect no sympathy from me. Because you have the power to take control of your life and you've got to stop regarding yourself as a victim. Feeling sorry for yourself will get you nowhere. See this glowing coal I hold in my

hands. Its glow is a manifestation of the glow that is within us all and that's why it can do no harm. It comes from the everlasting fire. I'm going to take it and place it in your heart. Its glow will sustain and guide you through the dark days and empower you to achieve the realization of your dreams." You believe so you feel no pain as Prometheus deftly opens your chest and places the coal within you. What you feel is the power that is your birthright returning to you, the power that you thought you had lost. Take a minute of clock time, equal to all the time you need, to feel the glow spreading through your body as it charges you with power from the eternal source, the source that you lost your connection with but the source that you now know you are truly part of .....

Now the time has come to return to your everyday life. But you return with an inner glow of strength, secure in the knowledge that it can never be extinguished. Hold on to this precious gift and it will stand you in good stead. And when you return you'll remember these words.

You look around you to find that you are alone. Prometheus, having accomplished his mission, has now moved on. Take this opportunity to give thanks and to survey the scenery all around you, the treasures that lie below in all four directions, the world of opportunities that awaits you. And take a minute of clock time, equal to all the time you need, to consider what use you will make of your gift ......

The time has now come for you to make your way back, back down the steps that lead through the core of mountain, back, back, through time and actuality, back through the gateway between the two worlds and back to the dawning of new day that is waiting for you on the other side. And so you step out of the cave into the daylight, ready for the new life that lies ahead of you.

Open your eyes, stretch your arms and legs and stamp your feet on the ground to make sure you're really back home again.

Fire ceremonies can be created as a means of letting go of what no longer serves us – self-destructive behaviour or damaging relationships. As with all forms of ceremony, the rituals are much more likely to have an impact if they are created by the participants themselves instead of being imposed upon them. In this way the clients taking part in the process have an opportunity to express their uniqueness and individuality. Sometimes the participants may be invited to reflect on what they would like to let go of, and to write it on a piece of paper or to create a piece of craftwork to represent the wish. With everyone sitting in a circle in the open air around a fire, chanting might be used to raise the energy level and bring the group together. The members of the group might then take it in turns to approach the fire with their slips of paper and to talk to the Spirit of the Fire, asking it to accept the request or to fulfil the wish and to transform the weakness into strength. The symbol is then placed in the flames and burnt. This could be followed by the creation of a symbolic object which represents all the clients future hopes. This is an item to be treasured. It can be kept in an honoured place such as on a personal altar or in a pouch hung around the neck .

THE HOLY FIRE

Come to me I offer comfort
Prepare yourself for what's to come
The seagulls circle overhead
So take heed of their warning cries

Take your courage in both hands
And step into the holy fire
Allow yourself to be transformed
In the flames that hold your future

Let go of the past you cling to
Allow the new to take its place

123

Have no fear of stepping into
The unknown you've always yearned for

You who have lived just half a life
You who have tied yourself up in knots
It's time you took your rightful place
And realized your full potential

In most of the world religions there is a **Festival of Light** and the equation of light with goodness is a universal metaphor. From the Zoroastrian wheel of fire to the Advent candle, light is seen as a purifying force and a weapon against the powers of darkness. It is this symbolism which gives the festivals of light their power.

Diwali is probably the most widely celebrated of all the Hindu festivals and it is also an important festival for Sikhs. The word "Diwali" actually means a garland of light. There is also the Jewish festival of Hanukkah to commemorate the miracle that kept the lamp burning bright in the Temple reclaimed from Antiochus of Syria. Despite the fact that there was only enough oil left to last for one day, it miraculously burnt for eight until new supplies of oil arrived. Every Bhuddhist country has a festival of light too. The Thai festival, for example, takes place in November and is celebrated with fireworks and offerings of floating candles to the river spirits.

In the cold northern regions, the festival falls in Autumn or mid-winter because that's the time when the sun needs our help. The Celts called this season Samhain, or Summer's End, and saw it as a time of death and new beginnings. Each year, the high king of Ireland took part in a ceremony in which he was ritually slain by wounding, burning and drowning and then seen to come to life again to rule for another year.

According to Celtic belief, this was the time when ghosts walked abroad and the Lord of Death unleashed his demons on the world, so the Celts kept their house fires burning all night long on Samhain Eve (October 31) They also kindled great bonfires (originally "bone fires") to strengthen the dying sun.

The Christian church could not ignore this all-important festival so November 1 became All Saints Day. However, the old Celtic belief survived in the tradition that spirits walk abroad on the eve of All Saints Day, or Halloween. It was customary to set out gifts of soul cakes and wine for the visiting dead and from this tradition springs the modern custom of "trick or treating".

Nobody knows when the custom of making Halloween lanterns began, but sources show that country people were hollowing out mangel-wurzels (a type of beet) to make tallow lanterns as early as Elizabethan times. In Hinton St, George, Somerset, they call them punkies and to this day the children of the village celebrate Punkie Night every year.

BY A REPORTER FROM ANOTHER PLANET

Every morning it would be there for all to see but nobody bothered to notice. They would even cover their eyes with dark glasses to avoid its glare. They would curse it for making them sweat, be resentful due to the fact that it teased them by often having a weekend break, blame it for bringing out the insects, accuse it of being responsible for producing yellow patches on the lawn, and even attribute defeats in cricket matches to it. It was blamed it for putting up holiday prices and for causing overcrowding on beaches and it was cited as the cause of both skin allergies and cancer. Some people even went so far as to intimate that it was a factor in producing early signs of aging – extra wrinkles on the skin.

In the end it got tired of being unappreciated and decided to up and go. Nobody blames it for anything any more. But that's because there's nobody left on this planet these days.

THE AGE OF REASON

The young man was tired. He'd tried everything. It had started with the religion he was born into, which he'd rejected as it only seemed to be the cause of conflict – different groups all saying they were the chosen ones and then fighting with each other. He'd then gone to the other extreme, rejecting everything, but found that unsatisfactory too as it left him feeling so disconnected. The next step in his quest for the answer was to register for various workshops given by the gurus that everyone bowed down to. Not only did they cost the earth but they seemed to be composed almost entirely of lonely middle-aged women looking for crutches to lean on. In desperation he even journeyed to an Ashram in India for an audience with a so-called enlightened being who turned out to be nothing more than a second-rate street magician. And all he came back with was a severe bout of food poisoning and an even more worrying overdraft.

He came to the conclusion that it had all been a complete waste of time. The sole aim of all the teachers he'd encountered along the way had been to disempower the poor miserable souls who came to them in search of enlightenment. However, he had the sense to realise they weren't solely to blame for the situation as they were entirely dependent on the lack of self-belief of their followers for their success.

And so he'd reached the crossroads. Who to turn to next? Of all the people he met on a daily basis, there was only one who seemed to have peace of mind. And that was the local newsagent he bought his newspaper from each morning on his way to work. So, as a last resort, he decided to approach him in attempt to find out what made him tick.

"Help me. I want to be able to believe but find myself unable to. I look around and see so much injustice and suffering that it destroys my faith. How do you manage to always be so upbeat? What's your secret?" However, as soon as he found himself saying these words, he instantly regretted his rash decision to take such a step. The newsagent probably thought he was a lunatic who'd escaped from a local asylum. He was about to beat a hasty retreat when the wise old soul placed a hand upon his shoulder and stopped him.

"Come outside with me and I'll show you something that will make you change your mind." The young man followed him out of the shop as if in a trance. Now look up at the sun with your eyes open wide. "But I can't!" The student protested.

"Exactly," the wise old soul replied. "The sun is just God's messenger and you can't bear to look at him. So just imagine what the power of God himself must be like. Of course there's a great deal that you can't understand and that I can't either. In fact, it's pointless even attempting to do so. All we need to do is to let that power flow through us and trust in the process." And that's when the young man grew up.

WATER

The ancient philosophers regarded water as a basic element typifying all liquid substances and scientists did not discard that view until the latter half of the 18th century. In 1781 the British chemist Henry Cavendish synthesized water by detonating a mixture of hydrogen and air. However, the results of his experiments were not clearly interpreted until two years later, when the French chemist Antoine Laurent Lavoisier proposed that water was not an element but a compound of oxygen and hydrogen.

It is in the ground and in our bodies, in the seas and in the skies. It rots our houses and floods our streets, feeds our crops and can be found in our parks and gardens. Way back in evolution, we crawled out of it. Before we're born we spend nine months suspended in it. We may work on it, rest in it or play in it, but most of all we depend on it because without water we would not be here.

WHY THE SUN AND MOON LIVE IN THE SKY

Many years ago the sun and the water were the best of friends, and both lived on the earth together. The sun very often used to visit the water, but the water never returned his visits. At last the sun asked the water why it was that he never came to see him in his house. The water replied that the sun's house was not big enough, and that if he came with his people he would drive the sun out.

The water then said, "If you'd like me to visit you, you must build a very large compound; but I warn you that it will have to be a tremendous place, as my people are very numerous and take up a lot of room."

The sun promised to build a very big compound, and soon afterwards he returned home to his wife, the moon, who greeted him with a broad smile when he opened the door. The sun told the moon what he had promised the water, and the next day he started building a huge compound to entertain his friend in.

When it was completed, he asked the water to come and visit him the next day.

When the water arrived, he called out to the sun and asked him whether it would be safe for him to enter, and the sun answered, "Yes, come in, my friend."

The water then began to flow in, accompanied by the fish and all the water animals.

Very soon the water was knee-deep, so he asked the sun if it was still safe, and the sun again said, "Yes," so more water came in.

When the water was level with the top of a man's head, the water said to the sun, "Do you want more of my people to come?"

The sun and the moon both answered, "yes," not knowing any better, so the water flowed in, until the sun and moon had to perch themselves on the top of the roof.

Again the water addressed the sun, but, receiving the same answer, and more of his people rushing in, the water very soon overflowed the top of the roof, and the sun and the moon were forced to go up into the sky, where they have remained ever since. (adapted from Radin, P., 1983)

Sometimes a stretch of water can act as a barrier or a source of division, especially when the people involved in the matter have tunnel vision and walk around wearing blinkers over their eyes! Khelm is the equivalent of Gotham in British folktales – the place where stupid people are supposed to live:

A BRIDGE IN KHELM

A river flowed right through the middle of Khelm. It occurred to several merchants that a bridge over it would be good for business on both sides of the river. But some of the younger people objected. They said: "Of course it would be nice to build a bridge, but let's not do it because it would be good for business; we should build it solely for aesthetic reasons. We'd be glad to contribute towards the cost for beauty's sake, but we won't give a penny for the sake of trade." Still others, even younger people, said, "A bridge! That's a good idea, but not for the sake of trade or beauty but to have some place to stroll back and forth. We'd be glad to contribute money to build a bridge for strolling, but not for any other reason." And so the three groups began to quarrel, and they are quarreling still. And to the present day Khelm still does not have a bridge.

As water typically moves downwards, its emergence from the earth is taken to represent a sacred gift from the womb of the Earth Mother. **Well Dressing ceremonies** still take place in England and the miraculous healing powers of water from wells are legendary. Moreover, given the importance of water to farming communities, it is hardly surprising that wells feature so frequently in folk tales:

THE MIRACLE OF THE DRY WELL

The Rebbe of Vizhnits, Reb Mendele, was being driven out of his mind by a man who complained that he had built a house and bricked in a well, and it had cost him a great deal of money, but there was no water in the well. One day the Rebbe said to him, When I travel to Kosev to visit Reb Khaim, the route I take will be near your house. Remind me then."

When the time came for the journey, the Rebbe passed near the man's house at about the time of early evening prayers. The Rebbe interrupted his journey and said to the man, "I want to wash my hands. Dip up a ladle of water from your well for me."

"But Rebbe, the well is dry," said the man

"Don't be a fool. Have you ever seen a well without water? Take your ladle and dip." Since it was the Rebbe's command, the man did as he was told, and indeed drew up a ladle of water. The Rebbe washed his hands. "Now dip up a cup of water, I want a drink, too." The man drew up a full cup of water. The Rebbe drank – and from that time on there was always water in the well.

The Hopi American Indians believe it is absolutely essential to have the supernaturals on their side. The Hopis feel that their supernaturals have certain powers which they do not have, and that they in turn possess things which their supernaturals desire. Thus often Hopi rituals are mutual gift-

130

giving ceremonies. The Hopi Kachina dolls represent supernaturals, embodying the spirits of living things. Kachinas are believed to possess powers over nature, especially the weather, and are made use of in Rain Dance ceremonies. However, the Rain Dance is not only a feature of American Indian traditions. The drawing of the Circle in the dust in the following Israeli tale probably alludes back to earlier pagan practices:

HONI THE CIRCULAR

Many years ago the land was dry and everything was thirsty for water – the people, the trees and the animals. The rainy season of the year came and past, without a single drop, and the people were getting worried. There were no clouds to be seen in the sky and not even a single gust of wind to give them hope. Every morning the people looked up to the heavens and prayed but the land continued to remain as dry as a bone.

Honi was a peaceful man. The people said, "Honi will make it rain for us." So they went to Honi and asked him: "Can you make it rain for us?" Honi took a stick, drew a circle around himself in the dust, and prayed: "God please give us rain." and that's when it started. Just a few drops at first. So Honi said, "God please give us a bit more – it's not enough" and that's when it came down in buckets.

And that's why they call him Honi the circular.

Ritual washing in water, or immersion in a pool, has been part of various religious systems since the beginning of time. The priests of ancient Egypt washed themselves in water twice each day and twice each night; in Siberia, ritual washing of the body -- accompanied by certain chants and prayers -- was a part of shamanic practices. In Hindu, "ghats" are traditional sites for public ritual bathing, an act by which one achieves both physical and spiritual purification. In strict Jewish households, hands must be washed before saying

131

prayers and before any meal including bread; in Islam, mosques provide water for the faithful to wash before each of the five daily prayers. In Christian tradition, baptism is described by St. Paul as 'a ritual death and rebirth which simulates the death and resurrection of Christ.'

According to Mircea Eliade, 'The Waters ... are ... the reservoir of all the potentialities of existence; they precede every form and sustain every creation. ... Emergence repeats the cosmogonic act of formal manifestation; while immersion is equivalent to a dissolution of forms. That is why the symbolism of the Waters includes Death as well as Re-Birth' (Eliade, M., 1952, p.151). 'In whatever religious context we find them, the Waters invariably preserve their function: they dissolve or abolish the forms of things, "wash away sins", are at once purifying and regenerative. ... The purpose of the ritual lustrations and purifications is to gain a flash of realisation of the non-temporal moment ... in which the creation took place; they are symbolical repetitions of the birth of worlds or of the "new man" ' (*Ibid.* p.152).

The water element can be used to clean out negativity. If Frog is hopping by your side, you may be in need of a cleansing time. Hop into the water, relax and take deep cleansing breaths. You are capable of immersing yourself and transforming your life in much the same way as a tadpole becomes a Frog.

Your Guide is talking again, this time leading you through the visualisation of a waterfall:

Take a few deep breaths to help you relax. Breathe in the light and breathe out all your tightness. Feel the tension disappear stage by stage from the top of your head to the tips of your toes. Let your surroundings fade away as you gradually sink backwards through time and actuality and pass through the gateway of reality into the dreamtime

You find yourself on a rocky path in the foothills of a mountain range. It's summer and the sun is beating down on you. You can hear the sound of fast-flowing water. You're following the course of a stream that runs alongside the path and your goal is to seek the source. The hot weather and the climbing make you thirsty so you stop to take a rest. You bend down, cup your hands together, place them in the stream and raise the water to your lips. The water tastes pure and sweet and it surges through your body like liquid crystal. Take a minute of clock time, equal to all the time you need, to savour the revitalising effects .....

And now the time has come for you to set off on your way again. The climb is arduous and the rocks are slippery but you're determined to reach your destination and will let nothing stand in your way. As you get closer, the sound of the water gets louder and the trickle you heard before is now a roar. Just then you turn a corner and find yourself face to face with your goal.

As a result of the exertions of the climb, you're feeling hot sticky so you strip off and immerse yourself in the source. You gasp as the icy cold torrents hit you but gradually you become acclimatised. You feel as if it's cleansing you to the very core, like no bath or shower has ever done before. Not only is it washing off the physical dirt but the spiritual dirt you've accumulated too. It's as if you're being reborn. Take a minute of clock time, equal to all the time you need, to appreciate what it feels like to be unburdened and renewed .....

Now you move behind the curtain of water, to where you're cut off from the outside world, alone, just you and your inner voice, with no distractions. Take a minute of clock time, equal to all the time you need, to listen to what your inner voice is saying, the message it has especially for you - for the well-being of both your body and your soul ......

Cleansed of the negativity you were carrying around with you and enlightened by the words of wisdom you heard, the time has now come to make your way home. And as you retrace your steps down the path, alongside the fast-flowing stream, you know you're returning to make a fresh start in the everyday world you left behind you, replenished with energy and a new sense of purpose. You give thanks for the healing and insights you've received as you continue to return, back along the path, back through the gateway between the two worlds, and back to the place you started from.

> Legend says that the River Piedra is so cold that anything that falls into it – leaves, insects, the feathers of birds – is turned to stone. Maybe it would be a good idea to toss your suffering into its waters. (Coelho,P., 2000)

The idea of regeneration through water can be found in numerous pan-cultural tales about the miraculous **Fountain of Youth**. So pervasive were these legends that in the 16th century the Spanish conquistador Ponce de Leon actually set out to find it once and for all -- and found Florida instead. In Japanese legends, the white and yellow leaves of the wild chrysanthemum confer blessings from Kiku-Jido, the chrysanthemum boy who dwells by the Fountain of Youth. These leaves are ceremonially dipped in *sake* to assure good health and long life. One Native American story describes the Fountain of Youth created by two hawks in the nether-world between heaven and earth. Those who drink of it outlive their children and friends, which is why it is eventually destroyed.

Water has always been associated with purification. In Hindu belief, rivers symbolize purification and the Ganges can wash away all your shortcomings. The same association can be found in the work of Shakespeare too. There is the example of Lady Macbeth, tortured with guilt, trying to wash the bloodstains off her hands. The following Yiddish folktale echoes that theme. Although the story refers to those who have spilt Jewish blood, its message is universal and it can be applied to all who are guilty of crimes against humanity:

BLOOD AND WATER

Once upon a time there was a King who went to a river to bathe. When he came to its bank, he saw that half of the stream was water but the other half was blood. And there was a man in the middle trying to cross over from the blood to the water.

The King was puzzled by this so he called together all the priests, rabbis, and other holy folk to ask them what it meant. But none of them could see anything in the river but water and they could only come to the conclusion that the King was seeing things and that perhaps he was suffering from stress.

But the King was not convinced. So he sent for the greatest rabbi in the city, and this rabbi saw exactly what the King had seen. And this was his interpretation:

"Half of the river is the blood that has been spilled," said the rabbi, "And the other half is the tears that Jews have wept." The man in the middle is your father, who is trying to cross from hell into paradise. But to do this he must wade out of the Jewish blood he has shed, and the river will not let him."

Water can also be used to awaken the powers of intuition. Coelho suggests the following exercise to facilitate the process:

THE AROUSAL OF INTUITION
(The Water Exercise)

Make a puddle of water on a smooth, non-absorbent surface. Look into the puddle for a while. Then, begin to play with it, without any particular commitment or objective. Make designs that mean absolutely nothing.

Do this exercise for a week, allowing at least ten minutes each time.

Don't look for practical results from this exercise; it is simply calling up your intuition, little by little. When this intuition begins to manifest itself at other times of the day, always trust in it. (Coelho, P., 1997)

Stories of great floods seem to be common to most cultures. The Old Testament story of Noah was derived from the earlier Gilgamesh Epic of the Baylonians. And the Babylonian version in turn drew on a pre-existing flood myth that no doubt went back thousands of years earlier. So old is the **Flood myth**, in fact, that it has had a chance to diffuse far and wide. Indeed, it is known to practically every human society from aboriginal Australia to Tierra del Fuego. The Incas of Peru had their own Noah story in which a man and a woman survive by floating in a box; while in an Indian myth, Manu is warned of a deluge by fish, builds a boat, lands on one of the Himalayan peaks and goes on to father mankind via an incestuous union with his daughter. However, the near-universality of a flood story is no more proof that a flood once covered the earth than the widespread belief in a Fall-of-the-Sky myth is proof that the sky once actually fell.

The following Creation Myth is an American Indian version in which the location of the flood is geographically specific. The ending seems somewhat inconclusive and one is left to wonder what the next means of reducing the population of the world will be:

THE GREAT FLOOD

In ancient times, there were so many people in the land that they lived everywhere. Soon hunting became bad and food scarce, so that the people quarrelled over hunting territories.

Even in those days, the people were skilled in making fine canoes and paddles from cedars, and clothing and baskets from their bark. In dreams their wise old men could see the future, and there came a time when they all had similar bad dreams that kept coming to them over and over again. The dreams warned of a great flood. This troubled the wise men who told each other about their dreams. They found that

136

they all had dreamed that rain fell for such a long time, or that the river rose, causing a great flood so that all of the people were drowned. They were much afraid and called a council to hear their dreams and decide what should be done. One said that they should build a great raft by tying many canoes together. Some of the people agreed, but others laughed at the old men and their dreams.

The people who believed in the dreams worked hard building the raft. It took many moons of hard work, lashing huge cedar log canoes together with strong ropes of cedar bark. When it was completed, they tied the raft with a great rope of cedar bark to the top of Mount Cowichan by passing one end of the rope through the centre of a huge stone which can still be seen there.

During the time when the people were working on the raft, those who did not believe in the dreams were idle and just laughed at their efforts. Even so, those very same people could not help but admire the fine, solid raft when it was at last finished and floated in Cowichan Bay.

Soon after the raft was ready, huge raindrops started falling, rivers overflowed, and the valleys were flooded. Although people climbed Mount Cowichan to avoid the great flood, it too was soon under water. But those who had believed the dreams took food to the raft and they and their families climbed into it as the waters rose. They lived on the raft many days and could see nothing but water. Even the mountain tops had disappeared beneath the flood. The people became much afraid when their canoes began to flood and they prayed for help. Nothing happened for a long time; then the rain stopped.

The waters began to go down after a time, and finally the raft was grounded on top of Mount Cowichan. The huge stone anchor and heavy rope had held it safe. As the water gradually sank lower and lower, the people could see their lands, but their homes had all been swept away. The valleys and forests had been destroyed. The people went back to their old land and started to rebuild their homes.

137

After a long time the number of people increased, until once again the land was filled and the people started to quarrel again. This time they separated into tribes and clans, all going to different places. And the storytellers say this is how people spread all over the earth.

From a ceremonial point of view, as has already been pointed out, Water has always played a cleansing role. In the Christian ritual of **baptism** a small portion of the original essence of pagan practices can still be found. It is said that the newborn human being is washed free of original sin with baptism. Sin can be regarded as the separation from the Original Oneness. The water of baptism is holy water that heals by pervading us with the power of the eternally flowing current of life. It also reminds us that within us too flows this spirit and that it is possible for us to merge spiritually with the Whole even while we are here on earth. The shaman works with the cleansing power of water as a means of reuniting human beings with the Whole.

Now for another Yiddish folktale, and a warning to take everything you hear from the so-called experts with a pinch of salt!

WATER WOULDN'T HURT

An exhausted disciple came running to his Holy Man. "Teacher, help. Take pity. My house is burning."
The Holy Man calmed his disciple. Then, fetching his staff from a corner of the room, he said, "Here, take my staff. Run back to your house. Draw circles around it with my staff, each circle some seven handbreadths from the other. At the seventh circle, step back seven handbreadths, then lay my staff down at the east end of the fire."
The disciple hurriedly noted the instructions down, grabbed the staff and started off. "Listen," the Holy Man called after him, "it wouldn't hurt also to pour on water. Yes, in God's name, pour on water. As much water as you can."

Moses as a Shaman and a Storyteller

In 1775 Johann Gottlieb Georgi suggested that shamanism was a very ancient and influential form of religious expression and that it derived directly from the religion of Moses, with which he thought shamanist tradition had much in common. Whether shamanism derived from the religion of Moses or whether Judaism derived from shamanism is not really of concern here. What is clear, however, is that there are not only definite parallels between the two but that in many respects Moses can be regarded as a shaman, as will be shown in the pages that follow.

> According to history, the Jewish religion began with the revelation of the Torah (Law) by God to Israel on Mount Sinai (Exodus 19:5-6). God appeared to Moses on the mountaintop, and there He revealed the laws and doctrines the children of Israel were to follow so that they might become a "holy nation." What was it that was revealed to Moses? Much more than the Ten Commandments! The reason why Moses spent "forty days and forty nights" before God on Mount Sinai was because Moses was receiving an extensive education in Divine Law and exactly how to apply that Divine law on the Earthly level for the Israelite people. Moses had to be able to give all the laws to the Levitical Priesthood, and explain to them exactly how to transform the Laws into actual physical application and practice. Also, Moses had to know exactly how to transform all the Laws for the entire Israelite nation into practical application and physical practice. This involved two sections of revealed Law: (1) the portion of Law to be written down and given to all Israel; and, (2) the esoteric or Oral Law to be memorized by Moses and the priests which would enable them to teach the people the technical level of the Law so the people could all obey the Law together in harmony according to God's will. According to history, Moses received the Oral Torah on

Mount Sinai and verbally transmitted it to Joshua. Joshua transmitted it to the elders, and the elders to the prophets, and the prophets to the members of the Great Assembly' (Whitaker, D., *"The Oral Torah"*, web article:1998)

That Moses must have been an accomplished storyteller (if we are to believe that the first five books of the Bible, the so-called Five Books of Moses, are actually works of hitory and autobiography authored by Moses himself) is clear from the fact that he achieved his goals and that he would never have been able to do so if he had not been able to effectively impart information through this form.

As Campbell points out, things have changed a great deal since the time of Moses and 'there is no divinely ordained authority any more that we have to recognize. There is no anointed messenger of God's law. In our world today all civil law is conventional. No divine authority is claimed for it: no Sinai, no Mount of Olives' (Campbell, J., 1973, p.248). Consequently, one of the problems that Judaism today has to contend with is that what is being presented is perceived by many as no longer being relevant. Of course Judaism is not alone in this respect as the same applies to other religious traditions too.

> The books of Exodus and Leviticus contain an account of the series of face-to-face meetings between Yahweh and Moses (Fourteenth to Thirteenth century BC) on Mount Sinai which yielded not only the enormously influential Ten Commandments, but also the Laws of Kosher or ritual purity, still observed by pious Jews. This kind of encounter between mortal and divine, involving a difficult ascent by the former, is plainly shamanistic (Rutherford, W., 1986, pp.136-137).

It is also worth noting that

> gematrically, the word "Sinai" is equal to the Hebrew word
> for "ladder". That is to say, if the letters making up each
> word are read as numbers their sum is the same in both
> cases. This would be no more than a coincidence were it not
> that the two interchangeable images lie at the heart of
> Kabbalism. One is the tree; the other, the ladder, both
> common metaphors for the shaman's journey. ... the
> gematric correspondence between Sinai, repeatedly referred
> to in scripture as "the Holy" or "God's Mountain", and the
> ladder is no coincidence; it is the key to the passages in
> Exodus and Leviticus, and tells us that Moses's visits to the
> mountain are, indeed, shamanic ascents. (*Ibid.* pp.137-138)

Let me prefix the account of the life of Moses that follows by
quoting from the end of the story, Deuteronomy 34: 10: 'And
there arose not a prophet since in Israel like unto Moses, whom
the Lord knew face to face'. In fact, Moses is the only man in
the Hebrew Bible to encounter God 'face to face.'
Consequently, the importance of Moses in the history of
religion for both Jews and Christians cannot be overstated.
However, my main concern here is to focus on Moses as both a
shaman and a storyteller.

Lewis, quoting Butt, explains how 'the shaman has
many roles, ranging from doctor, military tactician, and priest
to lawyer and judge: at one and the same time he is the
primitive embodiment of the National Space Agency and the
Citizen's Advice Bureau' (Lewis, I.M., 2003 Third Edition,
p.142). 'In this uncentralized society of small local groups
which have no other courts, the séance is a most important
mechanism for ventilating and bringing to a conclusion
smouldering quarrels and enmities' (*Ibid.* p.144). Religious
leaders have similarly performed social good 'by checking
within tribes the tendencies to internal warfare. ... The reproof
of Moses to the Israelite who struck a brother slave in Egypt,

"Wherefore smitest thou thy fellow?" will occur to the reader as an illustration of this point' (Maddox, 2003, p.287). This incident occurred early on in the life of Moses: Exodus, Chapter 2: 13.

From an early age Moses was gifted with visions, recorded by anthropologists as being a common occurrence among those destined to become shamans. The first reference to such a vision can be found in Exodus 3: 2: 'And the angel of the Lord appeared unto him in a flame of fire out of the midst of a bush: and he looked, and, behold, the bush burned with fire, and the bush was not consumed'. As Eliade points out, '"Seeing" a spirit, either in dream or awake, is a certain sign that one has in some sort obtained a "spiritual condition," that is, one has transcended the profane condition of humanity' (Eliade, 1964, p.85).

According to Otto, creature-consciousness 'is the emotion of a creature, submerged and overwhelmed by its own nothingness in contrast to that which is supreme above all creatures' (Otto, R., 1958, p.10). 'For the 'creature-feeling' and the sense of dependence to arise in the mind the 'numen' must be experienced as present' (*Ibid.* p.11). 'It is especially in relation to this element of majesty or absolute overpoweringness that the creature-consciousness … comes upon the scene, as a sort of shadow or subjective reflection of it. … And this forms the numinous raw material for the feeling of religious humility' (*Ibid.* p.20). The consciousness of creaturehood can be seen as 'a self-depreciation which comes to demand its own fulfilment in practice in rejecting the delusion of selfhood, and so makes for the annihilation of the self' (*Ibid.* p.21). This must surely be what Moses experienced by the burning bush, and on the many other occasions when he was witness to God's power. The word 'numinous' stands for that aspect of deity which eludes comprehension in rational or ethical terms, and 'there is no religion in which it does not live as the real innermost core, and without it no religion would be worthy of the name' *(Ibid.* p.6).

Otto observes that 'in religion there is very much that can be taught – that is, handed down in concepts and passed on in school instruction. What is incapable of being so handed down is this numinous basis and background to religion, which can only be induced, incited, and aroused' *(Ibid.* p.60). This numinous basis is the foundation of shamanism, which is why it is so difficult to put into words that can make sense to someone who has never had an experience of this nature.

'A definition of hierophancy may be established as any element of the experiential world of humanity which is perceived in such a way as to constitute a revelation of the sacred' (Rennie, B. S., 1996, p.15). For Moses, the burning bush was just such a perception. As Rennie points out, 'In tending to restrict our existence to the plane of the spatio-temporal, modern humanity has lost the ability to apprehend the meanings of other planes of existence as true expressions of our existential situation' *(Ibid.* p.54).

> Whoever is confronted with potency clearly realizes that he is in the presence of some quality with which in his previous experience he was never familiar, and which cannot be evoked from something else but which ... can be designated only by religious terms such as "sacred" and "numinous".
> (Van Der Leeuw, G. , 1938, pp. 47-48).

This must be what Moses experienced at the site of the burning bush even though there might well have been a scientific explanation for what had happened. In antiquity everything that happened 'could be conceived as a miracle, even when it followed a wholly natural course' *(Ibid.* p.567). For the primitive mind ... even the simple fact that it is raining may be a "marvel" of God *(Ibid.* p.568) as in the case of the burning bush which became the medium of revelation *(Ibid.* p.569).

According to William James, religious leaders throughout history have invariably been 'creatures of exalted emotional sensibility ... and frequently they have fallen into trances, heard voices, seen visions, and presented all sorts of peculiarities which are ordinarily classed as pathological. Often, moreover, these pathological features in their career have helped to give them their religious authority and influence' (James, 1982, pp.6-7). Moses would appear to have been no exception.

A founder can be defined as 'primarily a **witness** to revelation: he has seen, or has heard, something; "to the numen there pertains a seer". ... Then he speaks of his experience, and appears as **prophet**. ... Their doctrine ... possesses power only in so far as their whole life enters into the "founding": then they are **examples,** archetypes of the genuinely pious life replete with power. When, finally, they devote their entire existence to foundation, they are called **mediators**' (Van Der Leeuw, 1933, p.651). He then goes on to add that 'the foundation of the religion of the people of Israel is related in the story of the burning bush. ... the essential features are God speaking and the founder listening' (*Ibid.* p.652). So Moses was both a founder and a prophet. The prophet has been described as 'a mere tool of Power, "filled with the god" and emptied of himself – literally an "enthusiast" '(Van Der Leeuw, 1933, p.222).

Another characteristic Moses shared with the prospective future shaman of the tribe was his reluctance to pursue the path and his feelings of self doubt. We find evidence of this in Exodus 3: 11: And Moses said unto God, Who am I, that I should go unto Pharaoh, and that I should bring forth the children of Israel out of Egypt? 'When he finally understood God was recruiting him for a task that must have struck him as not only incredible but downright impossible, Moses spoke up boldly – and suggested that God ought to send someone else to do the job' (Kirsch, J., 1999, p.113). He also pointed out that he was 'slow of speech and of a slow tongue' (Exodus: 4:10).

To convince shamanists of their effectiveness as practitioners and of their powers, shamans found it helpful to perform 'tricks' for their followers, and Moses receives training from God in how to do this during his process of initiation. God show Moses how to turn his rod into a serpent, produce a leprous hand out of his jacket and to turn water into blood. Further examples of this training can be found in Exodus 14: 16 for example: 'But lift thou up thine rod, and stretch out thine hand over the sea, and divide it: and the children of Israel shall go on dry ground through the midst of the sea'. Exodus 14: 26 provides another example: 'And the Lord said unto Moses. Stretch out thine hand over the sea, that the waters may come again upon the Egyptians, upon their chariots, and upon their horsemen'.

It is important to note that at no time was Moses making use of his own power. He was acting as a channel, which is what shamans also claim to do. This is made clear in Exodus 16: 8: '… what are we? Your murmurings are not against us, but against the Lord …'

At the same time, all through the process of his initiation, Moses was also being trained to become a recorder of the people's history and a skilled storyteller. Evidence to support this hypothesis can be found in Exodus 17: 14: 'And the Lord said unto Moses, Write this for a memorial in a book, and rehearse it in the ears of Joshua: for I will utterly put out the remembrance of Amalek from under heaven'. In fact, as Kirsch points out, 'According to devout tradition, the first five books of the Bible, the so-called Five Books of Moses (or "Torah" in Jewish usage) are actually works of history and autobiography authored by Moses himself: "From the mouth of God to the hand of Moses," as the Sabbath liturgy of Judaism proclaims every time the Torah is read in a synagogue' (Kirsch, J., 1999, p.14).

The future shaman is often removed from society for the process of his initiation, just as Moses was. It is not until Exodus 18 Verse 5 that he is finally reunited with them: 'And Jethro, Moses' father in law, came with his sons, and his wife unto Moses in the wilderness, where he encamped at the mount of God'. Jethro then gives Moses a timely reminder of the importance of not using his own personal power in case he should exhaust himself. This can be found in Exodus 18: 17: And Moses' father in law said unto him, The thing that thou doest is not good. Exodus 18: 18: Thou wilt surely wear away, both thou, and this people that is with thee: for this thing is too heavy for thee; thou art not able to perform it thyself alone. Exodus 18: 19: Hearken now unto my voice, I will give thee counsel, and God shall be with thee: Be thou for the people to Godward, that thou mayest bring the causes unto God'.

It is interesting to note that 'According to a few intriguing clues buried in the Bible, Moses was tutored in the ways of magic by his father-in-law, ... who is plainly described as a pagan priest but who played a decisive role in the enlightenment of Moses and the destiny of the Israelites. It was Jethro, not Moses, who offered the very first sacrifice to Yahweh. According to a slightly revisionist reading of the Bible, Jethro [can be regarded] as a sorcerer and Moses was his apprentice' (Kirsch, J., 1999, pp.8-9). 'Moses, the ethical monotheist who supposedly purged Israel of superstition, comes across at moments as a "cult magician," and the Bible preserves a "peculiar duality," as Elias Auerbach puts it, a juxtaposition of "the loftiest and purest ideas" and "remnants of magical witchcraft" ' (*Ibid* p.237). It can be argued that elements of 'magical witchcraft' might have been incorporated into the story of Moses to make it more appealing to people familiar with the old ways or that Judaism can be seen to have marked a period of transition between the pagan and the monotheistic way.

According to Vitebsky, 'Certain patterns of shamanic thought seem to recur across a wide range of landscapes, in many diverse cultures and in many different social and political situations. These may be a survival from the earliest human sense of the divine. As more elaborate societies developed over time, other forms of religion arose and shamanic ideas were often eliminated or incorporated. They sometimes lie hidden within the major world religions' (Vitebsky, P., 2001, p.26). This would seem to be the case in Judaism, and the training Moses underwent both with God and his brother-in-law can be seen to have incorporated such elements.

> The term initiation in the most general sense denotes a body of rites and oral teachings whose purpose is to produce a decisive alteration in the religious and social status of the person to be initiated. In philosophical terms, initiation is equivalent to a basic change in existential condition; the novice emerges from his ordeal endowed with a totally different being from that which he possessed before his initiation; he has become **another** (Eliade, 1958, p. x).

Moses can clearly be seen to undergo such a transformation, from the self-doubting character we met in Exodus to the wise old soul we shall encounter later in Deuteronomy.

> Shamans … are separated from the rest of the community by the intensity of their own religious experience. In other words, it would be more correct to class shamanism among the mysticisms than with what is commonly called a religion … [it] represents, as it were, the mysticism of the particular religion. A comparison at once comes to mind – that of monks, mystics, and saints within Christian churches (Eliade, 1964, p.8).

It can be seen that this is another attribute that Moses shared with the shaman.

The ascent of mount Sinai by Moses in Exodus 19: 3 clearly parallels the shamanic journey to the Upper World to meet the Sacred Teacher: 'And Moses went up unto God, and the Lord called unto him out of the mountain, saying, Thus shalt thou say to the house of Jacob, and tell the children of Israel …' As Eliade explains, 'the novice during his initiation, or the shaman in the course of the séance, climbs the tree or the sacred pole [or a mountain]; and despite the variety of socio-religious contexts in which it occurs, the ascent always has the same goal – meeting with the Gods or heavenly powers, in order to obtain a blessing (whether a personal consecration, a favour for the community, or the cure of a sick person'. (Eliade, 1958, p.77). 'Ascending to Heaven represents one of the oldest religious means of personally communicating with the Gods, and hence of fully participating in the sacred in order to transcend the human condition' *(Ibid.* p.78).

As Eliade, points out, it would be wrong to identify the ascent of the shaman into Heaven with the ascension of Moses on mount Sinai, the Buddha, of Mohammed, or of Christ, as the actual content of these ecstatic experiences is different. However, 'this does not prevent the notion of transcendence from expressing itself universally by an image of elevation: the mystical experience, in whatever religion it may be cradled, always implies a **celestial ascension**' (Eliade, 1952, p.166).

This is how Van Der Leeuw interprets the significance of the momentous event:

> In the revelation of God upon Sinai … while the whole stress of the narrative falls on the intellectual and moral content of the revelation, nevertheless Moses and Aaron "see" the Lord. … So it was that the great revelation systems arose, whatever rites, myths and customs already subsisted in a community being proclaimed anew as "revelation". This certainly never happened without an actual revelatory experience of some

great founder – of a Moses, Mohammed, Zarathustra – enriching whatever had been previously received and invigorating this with fresh energy, and often indeed with a new spirit; and in this connection the extremely important task of the **mediator of revelation** is disclosed. (Van Der Leeuw, G., 1933, pp.570 -571).

'In cultures that have the conception of three cosmic regions – those of Heaven, Earth and Hell – the "centre" constitutes the point of intersection of those regions. It is here that the break-though on to another plane is possible and, at the same time, communication between the three regions' (Eliade, 1952, p.40). The symbol of a Mountain 'situated at the Centre of the World is extremely widely distributed. We may recall the Mount Meru of Indian tradition, Haraberezaiti of the Iranians, the Norse Himingbjor, the "Mount of the Lands" in the Mesopotamian tradition, Mount Tabor in Palestine (which may signify *tabbur* – that is, "navel" or *omphalos*), Mount Gerizim, again in Palestine, which is expressly named the "navel of the earth", and Golgotha which, for Christians, represented the centre of the world, etc' (Eliade, 1952, p.42). 'The summit of the Cosmic Mountain is not only the highest point on the Earth, it is the navel of the Earth, the point at which creation began. "The Holy One created the world like an embryo," affirms a rabbinical text. "As an embryo proceeds from the navel onward, so God began the creation of the world from its navel onward, and from thence it spread in different directions" ' (*Ibid.* pp.43-44).

As Van Der Leeuw explains,

with stones of any peculiar size and shape [including mountains] the firm subjective assurance of the presence of Power has ever been associated. When, for instance Jacob, his head "resting" on a stone, lay down to sleep and had his remarkable dream, he expressed himself thus – and purely empirically: "How dreadful is this place! This is none other

149

but the house of God, and this is the gate of heaven", and he took the stone and set it up for a pillar, anointing it with oil. Even if this narrative is aetiological, and intended to account for the worship of a remarkable stone, still it remains typical of the way in which stones can become most intimately incorporated in man's experience (Van Der Leeuw, 1938, pp.53-54).

The oldest heaven is in fact the mountain-top and, in the Old Testament, deity dwells on the mount as God appears to Moses on Sinai.

It is interesting to note that three days of ritual purification had to be completed before God would consent to appear, as Moses told the Israelites, and that only freshly laundered clothing was to be worn on the day of the visitation. "Come not near a woman," Moses warned the menfolk (Exod. 19:15). These preparations very much resemble those that would be conducted by a shaman before undertaking a 'journey' or performing a séance.

In Exodus 24: 7 we find Moses as the storyteller: 'And he took the book of the covenant, and read in the audience of the people: and they said, All that the Lord hath said will we do, and be obedient'. And in Exodus 24: 12 we see Moses in the role of the teacher: 'And the Lord said unto Moses, Come up to me into the mount, and be there: and I will give thee tables of stone, and a law, and commandments which I have written; that thou mayest teach them'. It is not uncommon for both the role of storyteller and teacher to be combined as they tend to overlap.

The shaman acts as a mediator between the people and the spirits just as Moses acts as a mediator between the people and God. In Exodus 32: 10 God expresses his anger: 'Now therefore let me alone, that my wrath may wax hot against them, and that I may consume them'. However, by Exodus: 32: 14 Moses has succeeded in placating him: 'And the Lord repented of the evil which he thought to do unto his people'. In fact, Moses was the only person to have direct access to God in this way. He nature of their unique relationship is clarified in Exodus 33: 11: 'And the Lord spake unto Moses face to face, as a man speaketh unto his friend'.

There is also evidence to suggest that on mount Sinai Moses was actually in the state of an ecstatic trance, just as a shaman may experience. This can be found in Exodus 34: 29 and 30: 'And it came to pass, when Moses came down from mount Sinai with the two tables of testimony in Moses' hand, when he came down from the mount, that Moses wist not that the skin of his face shone while he talked with him. And when Aaron and all the children of Israel, saw Moses, behold, the skin of his face shone; and they were afraid o come nigh him'. We learn from Deuteronomy 9: 9 that Moses 'abode in the mount forty days and forty nights' and that he' neither did eat bread nor drink water. We know from the published accounts recorded by anthropologists that preparation for trancework by shamans frequently involved abstinence of this kind.

The Penguin Dictionary of Psychology defines trance as: 'a condition of dissociation, characterized by the lack of voluntary movement, and frequently by automatisms in act and thought, illustrated by hypnotic and mediumistic conditions.' Trance states can be readily induced in most normal people by a wide range of stimuli, applied either separately or in combination. Time-honoured techniques include the use of alcoholic spirits, hypnotic suggestion, rapid over-breathing, the inhalation of smoke and vapours, music, and dancing, and the ingestion of such drugs as mescaline or lysergic acid and other psychotropic alkaloids ... Much the same effect can be produced, although usually in the nature of things more slowly, by such self-inflicted or externally imposed mortifications and privations as fasting and ascetic contemplation (e.g. 'transcendental meditation')' (Lewis, 2003, p.34).

According to William James, 'personal religious experience has its root and centre in mystical states of consciousness' (James, 1982, p.379). 'Four marks which, when an experience has them, may justify us in calling it mystical ... 1. **Ineffability**. ... The subject of it immediately says that it defies expression, that no adequate report of its contents can be given in words. It follows from this that its quality must be directly experienced; it cannot be imparted or transferred to others. ... 2. **Noetic quality**. ... mystical states seem to those who experience them to be also states of knowledge. They are states of insight into depths of truth unplumbed by the discursive intellect' (Ibid. p.380). 3. **Transiency**. - Mystical states cannot be sustained for long. ... 4. **Passivity**. - Although the oncoming of mystical states may be facilitated by preliminary voluntary operations, as by fixing the attention, or going through certain bodily performances, or in other ways which manuals of mysticism prescribe; yet when the characteristic sort of consciousness once has set in, the mystic feels as if his own will were in abeyance, and indeed sometimes as if he were grasped and held by a superior power' *(Ibid.* pp.380-381). Based on this definition, the experience Moses had on mount Sinai in the presence of God was clearly of a mystical nature.

One of the attributes of the shaman is the power of divination. Evidence that Moses was gifted with this attribute too can be found in Numbers 28: 12: And the Lord said unto Moses, Get thee up into this mount Abarim, and see the land which I have given unto the children of Israel. Numbers 28: 13: And when thou hast seen it, thou also shalt be gathered unto they people, as Aaron thy brother was gathered'. Not only was he allowed to know of his own death but also of the future of his people. This can be found in Deuteronomy 31: 16: And the Lord said unto Moses, Behold, thou shalt sleep with thy fathers; and this people will rise up, and go a whoring after the gods of the strangers of the land, whither they go to be among them, and will forsake me, and break my covenant which I have made with them'.

The shaman has also been known to fulfil a regulatory function, providing, through the séance, a mechanism of social control. This can be the case in societies which completely lack formal political officers, or courts of law, and where the shaman has virtually no rivals in his inspired ministrations.

> ... the most rudimentary society needs regulation if it is not to degenerate into anarchy. For instance, the human reproductive urge has to be regulated, a need which has led almost every society to surround sexual activity with complex taboos. ... It is the shaman who normally provides the regulatory mechanisms in the form of tribal laws whose original source will have been its totem which he alone is qualified to consult. Gradually a body of precedent and interpretation will be built up, passed on orally from one generation to the next (Rutherford, 1986, p.61).

It can be seen that this is clearly the role that Moses undertook for the people of Israel.

In Deuteronomy 4: 2 Moses gives the people the following instructions: 'Ye shall not add unto the word which I command you, neither shall ye diminish aught from it, that ye may keep the commandments of the Lord your God which I command you'. It is clear from this that there was to be no room for modification or innovation when it came to interpreting the laws. The neo-shamanic practitioners in our own times, who adopt such an eclectic approach to their methodology, would certainly not have met with the approval of Moses or his God!

By Dueteronomy 32: 2, the formerly reluctant representative of God, full of self doubt and feelings of unworthiness, has been transformed into the master storyteller, entrusted with teaching the children of Israel God's song: 'My doctrine shall drop as the rain, my speech shall distil as the dew, as the small rain upon the tender herb, and as the showers upon the grass'. By this stage, it is apparent that

Moses had become a master of his craft and had no need of his brother Aaron to support him. The man who had once claimed to be slow of speech delivers 'one last burst of oratory, a series of three speeches so lengthy and so ornate that the text takes up the entirety of the Book of Deuteronomy' (Kirsch, J., 1999, p.329).

> ... whoever encounters something peculiar cries: "my God" ... Power is thus authenticated and assigned a name; plural forms being intended to express the indeterminateness wherein the experience is more powerful than form creation. .. .The actual numinous experience itself is formless and structureless: it is the collision with Power, the encounter with Will (Van Der Leeuw, G., 1938, pp. 147-148).

> ... man longs to know the god's name; for only then can he begin to do something with his deity, live with him, come to some understanding and – in magic – perhaps even dominate him. The children of Israel, said Moses, will ask what is the name of Him that has sent him [Exodus iii. 13] *(Ibid.* pp.148-149).

It could be argued that Moses, recognizing this need, gave God a name or that God gave the people what they wanted through Moses, depending on whether you regard Moses as a storyteller or a mediator between God and the people. The third possibility is that he was in fact both. Whatever you decide upon, as Van de Leeuw points out, ' "god" is above all the name for some experience of Power' *(Ibid.* p.157).

It is important to point out at this stage that although it would not be inaccurate to say that Mohammed's ascension or, for that matter, Moses' vision quest on Mount Sinai, exhibit shamanic content, 'despite all the typological similarities, it is impossible to assimilate [something like] the ecstatic ascension of Mohammed to the ascension of an Altaic or Buryat shaman.

The content, the meaning, and the spiritual orientation of the prophet's ecstatic experience presuppose certain mutations in religious values that make it irreducible to the general type of ascension' (Eliade, 1989, p.377). However, pointing out the parallels between Moses and the figure of the shaman can provide us with "openings" into a trans-historical world, thus enabling the different "histories" to intercommunicate.

When Moses climbed Mount Sinai, he can be seen to have been embarking on a vision quest and what he returned with can be viewed as the teachings of his Sacred Teacher. Presumably he then had the problem of presenting these to the ordinary people in an understandable and tangible form and the symbol of the tablets provided the ideal vehicle for the purpose. 'Anything new and unknown causes distinct and even superstitious fear. The primitive manifests all the reactions of a wild animal to untoward events' (Jung, C.G., 1977 p.192). Moses, being a wise old soul, would surely have been aware of this. 'When a local history becomes sacred and at the same time ... a paradigm for the salvation of all humanity, it demands expression in a universally understandable language. But the only universal religious language is the language of symbols' (Eliade, M., 2003, p.119). The images of symbols 'give man a premonition of the divine while at the same time safeguarding him from immediate experience of it' (Jung, C.G., 1959, p.8).

On mount Sinai Moses can be said, in shamanic terms, to have acquired a guardian spirit, or at least to have further developed his relationship with one. 'The best-known way to acquire a guardian spirit is in a spirit quest in a remote place in the wilderness. The location may be a cave, the top of a mountain, [as in the case of Moses] or a tall waterfall or an isolated trail at night' (Harner, M., 1990 Third Edition, p.42). 'Without a guardian spirit it is virtually impossible to be a shaman, for the shaman must have this strong, basic power source in order to cope with and master the nonordinary or spiritual powers whose existence and actions are normally hidden from humans' (*Ibid.* p.43).

'It was possible, even in comparatively simple societies, for the select few to transform this journey into one with marked affiliations to the memorable journey of Dante, with its proper division into a via purgativa, a via illuminative, and a via unitiva and then ... to transfer it to this world so that the divine experience could become a preparation for the earthly experience and not the reverse' (Radin, P., 1957, p.166). This can be seen as what Moses achieved when he came down from Mount Sinai. 'Everywhere the priest-thinker has functioned in three ways: first, as a person with a special temperament and psychic make-up whose experiences have impressed themselves indelibly upon the form of religion and its constituent formulae; secondly, as an individual seeking for power and privileges who has invariably associated himself with those individuals or groups in his community striving for the same; and, thirdly, as a thinker attempting to bring order into the folkloristic background surrounding him on all sides' (*Ibid.* p.253). Moses can be said to have functioned in all these ways.

In conclusion, it is evident that storytelling was a tool that must surely have been used by shamans as a means of reaching the people, and was consequently an indispensable part of their repertoire, just as it was for religious figures such as Moses.

The question remains of how to **interpret** the story of Moses, literally or metaphorically. 'For the true believer in any of the Bible-based faiths – Judaism, Christianity, and Islam – the question of the "historicity" of Moses is faintly blasphemous. The Bible is the Received Word of God as given to Moses atop Sinai, or so goes a catechism that is common to all three faiths' (Kirsch, J., 1999, p.355). As Campbell points out, 'the peoples of all the great civilizations everywhere have been prone to interpret their own symbolic figures literally, and so to regard themselves as favoured in a special way, in direct contact with the Absolute. ... such literally read symbolic forms have always been – and still are, in fact – the supports of their civilizations, the supports of their moral orders, their cohesion, vitality, and creative powers' (Campbell, J., 1973, p.10). Consequently, they clearly have a very important part to play in maintaining the *status quo* within such traditions. However, they can also prove to be a divisive force in that they limit the dialogue possible with other traditions. If the Jews, for example, regard themselves as 'the chosen people,' how can they be non-judgemental of others? On the other hand, 'when these stories are interpreted ... as merely imagined episodes projected into history, and when they are recognized ... as analogous to like projections produced elsewhere, in China, India, and Yucatan, the import becomes obvious: namely, that although false and to be rejected as accounts of physical history, such universally cherished figures of the mythic imagination must represent **facts of the mind'** (*Ibid* p.12). However, what Campbell means by 'facts of the mind' is not at all clear. If by 'facts of the mind' he is referring to the way such stories portray the archetypal figures that Jung describes, then such figures can have a message for all of us and the significance of the biblical tales thus becomes universal.

It has to be said that given the fact that the name of Moses is not even mentioned in *The Song of Miriam*, generally believed to be the oldest fragment of the Bible, there has to be considerable doubt as to whether Moses ever existed. Reason to doubt the historicity of the story of Moses abound. For example,

> Some theologians are willing to speculate that the biblical depiction of God engaged in battle at the Red Sea harkens back to the old Canaanite myth. "[T]he sea crossing of the Exodus is being associated with the primordial act of creation," as Brevard Childs puts it. "Thus the victory over Pharaoh reflected the victory of order over the primordial

dragon of chaos, which was followed by the mythical battle with the sea." Even the use of a rod by Moses to part the waters is thought to recall a scene from Canaanite myth in which Baul uses a club to subdue the sea-god (Kirsch, J., 1999, pp.197-198).

The question also remains of why there is no mention of Moses in Egyptian records. 'The ancient Egyptians preserved everything from fishhooks to toilet seats – but nowhere in the archaeological record are the events of the Exodus or the existence of a man called Moses ever mentioned' (*Ibid* p.75). Another cause for doubt is the number of inconsistencies that can be found in the text. 'The mountain on which Moses encountered God in the burning bush is called Horeb in one passage – but the same mountain will later be called Sinai when Moses ascended to parley with God and came back down with the Ten Commandments ... This and other flaws in the biblical text suggest that the Bible was composed by combining and conflating a great many layers of storytelling from a great many sources' (*Ibid* p.126). However, as Kirsch himself points out, 'the saga of the Exodus is too unlikely – and Moses himself is ultimately too compelling – to have been merely a figment of some ancient storyteller's imagination' (*Ibid* p.22) and 'a life story so rich in detail and dialogue, so complex and full of contradiction, could [surely] not have been made up' (*Ibid* p.358). Moreover, whether the story is entirely based on fact, a mixture of fact and fiction, or entirely fictitious, there is no reason why this should detract from the way in which it has endured, the impact it has had, and the universal significance of its teachings.

If space allowed, the lives of other religious leaders involved in both journeying and storytelling could also be considered, including perhaps King Solomon. Among the Krekore Shona of the Zambesi Valley 'shamans are considered to deal with the moral order and with the relations of man to earth. ... Disputes are taken to him for settlement, as well as to the official secular courts, and he is also asked to decide issues concerning succession to chieftaincy and quarrels between neighbouring chiefs. In these matters it is the judgement of the guardian spirit, very properly sensitive to public opinion, that is delivered by the shaman' (Lewis, 2003, pp.122-123). This parallels the way in which King Solomon turned to God for guidance. As Butt, quoted in Lewis points out, the shaman 'has many roles, ranging from doctor, military tactician, and priest to lawyer and judge: at one and the same time he is the primitive embodiment of the National Space Agency and the Citizen's Advice Bureau' (Butt, 1967). Religious leaders from other traditions could also prove to be suitable cases for inclusion, such as Jesus, St. Paul or Mohammed.

As for the case for including Jesus, 'according to the Gospel account he appears to come into the full use of his powers [as a healer] only after his stay in the wilderness where he experienced a series of 'temptations'. ... Many commentators have also pointed out the death-and-rebirth elements in the Crucifixion and resurrection' (Rutherford, W., 1986, p.136). It is also interesting to note that 'The Dinka of southern Sudan, whose religion is in some ways reminiscent of the Old Testament, say that earth and sky were once very close together but that human misdeeds caused the sky to move far away so that bridging the gap has become a problem. In this light, Christ himself can be seen as a kind of shaman as he travels between heaven and earth in order to bring about the moral salvation of humanity' (Vitebsky, P., 2001, p.50).

'Very commonly, as with St Paul, the road to the assumption of the shaman's vocation lies through affliction, valiantly endured and, in the end, transformed into spiritual grace' (Lewis, 2003, p.60). 'The Chukchee ... compare the preparatory period in the assumption of the shaman's calling to a long and severe illness, and in fact the call of the spirits is often a direct consequence of an actual illness, misfortune, or danger. ... Among the Eskimo there are many ... accounts of

159

the rise to fame and fortune of shamans whose origins were full of misery and privation' (*Ibid*. p.61). 'Similar motifs … abound in our own culture. The New Testament traditions emphasize the lowly origin of the Carpenter of Nazareth and His early spiritual travails, particularly His temptation by the Devil on the mountain' (*Ibid*. p.62). 'By demonstrating his own successful mastery of the grounds of affliction … the shaman establishes the validity of his power to heal' (*Ibid*. pp.62-63).

Alchemists could also be considered, someone like Zosimus, for example:

> In the work of the alchemists … we find the ancient pattern of initiatory torture, death, and resurrection; but this time it is applied on an entirely different plane of experience - that of experimentation with mineral substance … Zosimus, one of the most important alchemists of the Hellenistic period, relates a vision that he had in a dream: a personage named Ion reveals to him that he (Ion) has been pierced by a sword, cut to pieces, beheaded, flayed, burned in fire, and that he suffered all this "in order that he could change his body into spirit." On awakening Zosimus wonders if all that he saw in his dream was not related to a certain alchemical process. In Ion's torture and cutting to pieces it is easy to recognize the pattern characteristic of shamanic initiations (Jung, C.G., 1968 2nd Edition, p.123).

The question of whether contemporary therapists such as Milton Eriksson or John Grinder can be regarded as both shamans and storytellers could also be explored. 'As Jung himself reminds us in his memoirs, in European culture the profession to which the conception of the wounded surgeon most poignantly and aptly applies is psychoanalysis. With this and other common features in mind, spirit possession and shamanism have also been viewed as a pre-scientific psychotherapy' (Lewis, 2003, p.172).

As it is, all these possible personages for consideration will have to wait until a sequel to this volume is written.

Jacob's Ladder, Jonah and the Whale

'Initiation represents a decisive experience for any individual who is a member of a pre-modern society; it is a fundamental existential experience because through it a man becomes able to assume his mode of being in its entirety' (Eliade, M., 2003, p.3). In this chapter it will be shown that both Jacob through his vision (the dream) and Jonah through his ritual death (when he was swallowed by the whale) can be said to have undergone such an experience.

Jacob was no saint. We learn in Genesis 25: 29 -31 that he was even prepared to exploit his own brother Esau by forcing him to sell his birthright when he was faint and in need of food. To make matters worse, his mother, Rebekah, encouraged him in his efforts to deceive his brother: 'Rebekah took goodly raiment of her Eldest son Esau, which were with her in the house, and put them upon Jacob her younger son' (Genesis 27: 15).Jacob then goes to his father, who is more or less blind, and says: 'I am Esau thy first born; I have done according as thou badest me: arise, I pray thee, sit and eat of my venison, that thy soul may bless me' (Genesis 27: 19). As a result, his father blesses him, believing he is in fact Esau: 'Therefore, God give thee of the dew of heaven, and the fatness of the earth, and plenty of corn and wine' (Genesis 27: 28).
So why did God choose Jacob to be his mediator? First of all, because there can be 'good' and 'bad' prophets in the same way as there can be 'good' and 'bad' shamans. However, perhaps more importantly, because Jacob later became a reformed character as we shall discover.

After deceiving Esau, Jacob had no choice but to flee, as God advised him to do, and it was then that he had the dream that was to change his life:

> And he lighted upon a certain place, and tarried there all
> night, because the sun was set; and he took of the stones of

that place, and put them for his pillows, and lay down in that place to sleep. And he dreamed, and behold a ladder set up on the earth, and the top of it reached to heaven: and behold the angels of God ascending and descending on it. And behold, the Lord stood above it, and said, I am the Lord God of Abraham thy father, and the God of Isaac: the and whereon thou liest, to thee I will give it, and to thy seed; And they seed shall be as the dust of the earth, and thou shalt spread abroad to the west, and to the east, and to the north, and to the south: and in thee and in thy seed shall all the families of the earth be blessed. And, behold, I am with thee, and will keep thee in all places whither thou goest, and will bring thee again into this land; for I will not leave thee, until I have done that which I have spoken to thee of. And Jacob awaked out of his sleep, and he said, Surely the Lord is in this place; and I knew it not. And he was afraid, and said, How dreadful is this place! this is none other but the house of God, and this is the gate of heaven. And Jacob rose up early in the morning, and took the stone that he had put for his pillows, and set it up for a pillar, and poured oil upon the top of it. And he called the name of that place Beth-el: but the name of that city was called Luz at the first. And Jacob vowed a vow, saying, If God will be with me, and will keep me in this way that I go, and will give me bread to eat , and raiment to put on, So that I come again to my father's house in peace; then shall the Lord be my God: And this stone, which I have set for a pillar, shall be God's house: and of all that thou shalt give me I will surely give the tenth unto thee (Genesis 28: 11-22).

The Talmud says "The dream is its own interpretation". However, some commentary would clearly be helpful at this point. 'The general function of dreams is to balance … disturbances in the mental equilibrium by producing contents of a complementary or compensatory kind,' (Jung, C.G., 1977, p.207) and this can be seen as the function of Jacob's dream. 'Most crises or dangerous situations have a long incubation, only the conscious mind is not aware of it. Dreams can betray the secret' (*Ibid.* p.208). As for the voice, 'The phenomenon of the "voice" in dreams ... expresses some truth or condition that is beyond all doubt', (Jung, C.G., 1968 2nd Edition, p.87) and in Jacob's dream the voice was God's.

> Many primitive peoples ... are familiar with an ascent to heaven on a ladder of arrows, while the ancient Egyptian Pyramid Texts depict the dead king as a bird, a falcon or goose, flying up to heaven, or climbing thither with ropes or an animal's skin, or a ladder (Van Der Leeuw, G., 1938, p.301).

Eliade, too, refers to the importance of such ascents: 'The act of climbing or ascending symbolises the way towards the absolute reality; and to the profane consciousness, the approach towards that reality arouses an ambivalent feeling. Of fear and of joy, of attraction and repulsion, etc.' (Eliade, 1952, p.51). Jung also refers to the significance of the theme of ascent: 'The initiations of late classical syncretism ... were particularly concerned with the theme of ascent, i.e., sublimation. The ascent was often represented by a ladder for the ka of the dead' (Jung, C.G., 1968 2nd Edition, pp. 57-58).

As Vitebsky and others have observed, a frequent motif in shamanic journeys is that of a **tree** or **ladder connecting earth and heaven**. He describes how 'the European story of Jack and the beanstalk closely resembles a *Yakut* shaman's rescue of the woman abducted as a prospective bride by the raven-headed people in the sky. The princess is captured and taken to the giant's castle in he clouds; Jack climbs up there, does battle with the giant and saves the princess. The main difference is that, as we now tell it, this story is not the foundation of a society and a system of morality' (Vitebsky, P., 2001, p.50).

The place where Jacob slept and had his dream was of great significance. 'According to Hebrew historians the original

Jewish centre of worship was not Jerusalem, but Mount Gerizim. It was only moved to the Temple Mount in Jerusalem after 980 BCE. Israelis refer to it as Har HaBayit, Hebrew for "temple mount" ' (Trubshaw, B., 2003, p.130). 'The sanctity of Temple Mount dates back over 4,000 years. According to Jewish legend, this was where Jacob slept and raised his stone, from which it was known as Bethel (from Beth El, 'House of God') (Genesis 28). It was where Abraham was commanded to sacrifice Isaac in a high place, Mount Moriah (about 2000 BCE). About a thousand years later David set up an altar at the place perceived to be the *'omphalos'* of the world (2 Samuel 24:21). Then, in about 960 BCE, Solomon erected the Temple of the Lord, 'His holy mountain, beautiful in elevation' (Psalms 48:2). 'And the altar of sacrifice was, again, the peak of Mount Moriah' (*Ibid*. pp.130-131).

> The famous Western (or Wailing) Wall, the last remnant of the second Jewish temple that the Romans destroyed in 70 BC, stands at the western base of the Temple Mount. Hebrew sources make it quite clear that Temple Mount is the centre of the world: 'Just as the navel is found at the centre of a human being, so the land of Israel is found at the centre of the world … Jerusalem is at the centre of the land of Israel, the Temple is at the centre of Jerusalem, the Holy of Holies is at the centre of the Temple, the Ark is the centre of the Holy of Holies, and the Foundation Stone is in front of the Ark, which spot is the foundation of the world (Midrash Tanhuma, Kedoshim 10) *(Ibid*. p.131).

It is of course not only in Judaism that mountains are considered to be sacred places. Mountains have long been prominent in religious cosmology in Japan too. 'They were regarded as the homes of powerful deities and the souls of the dead. Pilgrims to Mount Hiko ascend through four 'levels', each with increasing taboos (on the highest level there is a taboo on any bodily excretions such as urine, saliva, nasal

165

mucous). Time is considered to pass at a different speed at the different altitudes' (Trubshaw, B., 2003, p.124). The significance of mountains as sacred places in Japan is evident from the fact that 'it is from mountains that the medium summons both *kami*[2] and the benign dead. It is likewise in mountains that the ascetic looks for the other world from which he can gain the powers he desires' (Blacker, C., 1999, p.79). 'They are the abode both of the *kami* and of the dead' (*Ibid.* p.84).

How do we know about Jacob's Dream? Presumably he must have told the story to people, who then told it to others and/or recorded it, and, to do this, Jacob must have had a talent for telling stories or it would never have reached us as it has done. So it can be seen that, like Moses, Jacob must have been a storyteller too.

The dream sequence is followed by Jacob falling in love: 'And Jacob loved Rachel; and said I will serve thee seven years for Rachel thy younger daughter' (Genesis 29: 18). In the same way as Jacob had deceived his father, Rachel's father deceived Jacob, who was tricked into marrying Leah, Rachel's sister, first. However, in the end, he was rewarded for serving Laban by being able to marry Rachel too: 'And Jacob served seven years for Rachel; and they seemed unto him but a few days, for the love he had to her' (Genesis 29: 20). It is interesting to note the importance of the number seven and to recall that Thomas Rhymer in the ballad of the same name spent seven years in Elfinland.

The shaman acts as a channel for the power of the spirits just as the prophet acts as a channel for the words of God. Neither of them uses their own power. Jacob was clearly

---

[2] Motoori Norinaga, the great eighteenth century scholar of the Shinto revival, remarked that anything which was beyond the ordinary, other, powerful, terrible, was called '*kami*. ... they are able, freely and voluntarily, to cross the barrier which divides our world from theirs. This they may do of their own accord, irrupting suddenly and unexpectedly into our lives from another plane' (Blacker, C., 1999, pp.34-35).

aware of this as we learn from Genesis 30: 2: 'And Jacob's anger was kindled against Rachel: and he said, Am I in God's stead, who hath withheld from thee the fruit of the womb?' Let us turn now to Jacob's wrestling match:

> And Jacob was left alone: and there wrestled a man with him until the breaking of the day. And when he saw that he prevailed not against him, he touched the hollow of his thigh; and the hollow of Jacob's thigh was out of joint, as he wrestled with him. And he said, Let me go, for the day breaketh. And he said, I will not let thee go, except thou bless me. And he said unto him. What is thy name? And he said, Jacob. And he said, Thy name shall be called no more Jacob, but Israel: for as a prince hast thou power with God and with men, and hast prevailed. And Jacob asked him, and said, Tell me, I pray thee, thy name. And he said, Wherefore is it that thou dost ask after my name? And he blessed him there. And Jacob called the name of the place Peniel: for I have seen God face to face, and my life is preserved (Genesis 32: 24-30).

This can be interpreted as Jacob wrestling with his conscience, with his Inner Voice, or with God, and it is clearly a turning point in his life.

> The universal hero myth … shows the picture of a powerful man or god-man, who vanquishes evil in the form of dragons, serpents, monsters, demons, and enemies of all kinds, and who liberates his people from destruction and death. The narration or ritual repetition of sacred texts and ceremonies, and the worship of such a figure with dances, music, hymns, prayers, and sacrifices, grip the audience with numinous emotions and exalt the participants to identification with the hero. If we contemplate such a situation with the eyes of a believer, we can understand how the ordinary man is gripped, freed from his impotence and misery, and raised to an almost superhuman status, at least for the time being, and often enough he is sustained by such

167

a conviction for a long time. An initiation of this kind produces a lasting impression, and may even create an attitude that gives a certain form and style to the life of a society (Jung, C.G., 1977, pp.238-239).

According to Kirsch, Jacob's wrestling match with the angel (or was it God himself?) and his subsequent refusal 'to release his defeated opponent until he revealed his name [is] an incident that embodies "the age-old magical conception that knowledge of the right name confers on man some magic power , above all, power over the deity," as Auerbach explains. "That is why the deity is always evasive and does not give its name, nor will it hand his power over to man" ' (Kirsch, J., 1999, p.116). This is also explains why shamanic practitioners do not normally name their Power Animals or Spirit Helpers.

By this stage of the story, Jacob is clearly a reformed character, as can be seen from Genesis 35: 3: 'let us arise, and go up to Beth-el; and I will make there an altar unto God, who answered me in the day of my distress, and was with me in the way which I went.' And God appears to Jacob again and blesses him: 'And God said unto him, Thy name is Jacob: thy name shall not be called any more Jacob, but Israel shall be thy name: and he called his name Israel. And God said unto him, I am God Almighty: be fruitful and multiply; a nation and a company of nations shall be of thee, and kings shall come out of thy loins; And the land which I gave Abraham and Isaac, to thee I will give it, and to thy seed after thee will I give the land' (Genesis 35: 10-12).

This is followed by the story of Joseph. We learn that 'Israel loved Joseph more than all his children, because he was the son of his old age: and he made him a coat of many colours' (Genesis 37: 3). Even so, he was not blind to his faults, as we learn from Chapter 37 Verse 10: 'his father rebuked him, and said unto him, What is this dream that thou hast dreamed? Shall I and thy mother and thy brethren indeed come to bow down ourselves to thee to the earth?'

To cut a long story short, despite being sold into slavery by his brothers, Joseph eventually does very well for himself. Not only that, he also learnt from the mistakes he made along the way, as we find out when he forgives his brothers in Genesis 45: 4 – 9: 'I am Joseph your brother, whom ye sold into Egypt. Now therefore be not grieved, nor angry with yourselves, that ye sold me hither: for God did send me before you to preserve life. For these two years hath the famine been in the land: and yet there are five years, in the which there shall neither be earing nor harvest. And God sent me before you to preserve you a posterity in the earth, and to save your lives by a great deliverance. So now it was not you that sent me hither, but God: and he hath made me a father to Pharaoh, and lord of all his house, and a ruler throughout all the land of Egypt. Haste ye, and go up to my father, and say unto him, Thus saith thy son Joseph, God hath made me lord of all Egypt: come down unto me, tarry not.'

Jacob, on hearing the news, obviously wanted to go and see his beloved son before he died, but he was apprehensive about undertaking such a journey. However, God appeared to him once again to reassure him: 'And God spake unto Israel in the visions of the night, and said, Jacob, Jacob. And he said, Here am I. And he said, I am God, the God of thy father: fear not to go down into Egypt; for I will there make of thee a great nation' (Genesis 46: 2-3).

We learn from Genesis 47: 28 that 'Jacob lived in the land of Egypt seventeen years: so the whole age of Jacob was an hundred forty and seven years.' Specific details such as these serve the purpose of giving the story more credibility.

Just as Jacob's father had blessed the younger of the two brothers, Jacob did the same, but intentionally, with Joseph's sons: 'And Joseph said unto his father, Not so, my father: for this is the firstborn; put thy right hand upon his head. And his father refused, and said, I know it, my son, I know it: he also shall become a people, and he also shall be great: but truly his younger brother shall be greater than he, and his seed shall become a multitude of nations' (Genesis 48: 18-19). And so the story comes full circle, to the end of Jacob's life. However, Jacob's last act, before his death, was to inform his sons of what would happen to them. Like the shaman, Jacob was gifted with the power of divination, as we can see from Genesis 49: 1: 'And Jacob called unto his sons, and said, Gather yourselves together, that I may tell you that which shall befall you in the last days.'

As Eliade points out,

> In the archaic cultures communication between sky and earth is ordinarily used to send offerings to the celestial gods and not for a concrete and personal ascent; the latter remains the prerogative of shamans. Only they know how to make an ascent through the "central opening"; only they transform a cosmo-theological concept into a **concrete mystical experience**. This … explains the difference between … the religious life of a … people and the religious experience of its shamans; the latter is a **personal and ecstatic experience**. … Only for the latter is **real communication** among the three cosmic zones a possibility (Eliade, 1964, p.265).

The same clearly applies to the religious experiences of prophets like Jacob.

Although the Book of Jonah is one of the smallest in the Old Testament – only four chapters and forty-eight verses – its importance is evident from the fact that it is read on *Yom Kippur*, the holiest day of the year for the Jewish people.

It would seem that Jonah had been destined for greatness. 'The prophet Elijah was dispatched to Tzorfas where, he was told, a widow would provide for him (I Kings 17:9). He went and found a woman who was so poor that she was convinced that both she and her young son would soon die of starvation. Although Elijah blessed her with a miraculously inexhaustible supply of food, not long afterward, the child became ill and died. Elijah then tenderly took the child and carried him up to the little attic provided him by the widow, laid him on the bed she had given him, and pleaded with God to revive him. The child came back to life and Elijah returned him to his grateful mother. ... The young Jonah became Elijah's disciple and, when Elijah ascended to heaven, Jonah became the disciple of Elijah' (Scherman, N. & Zlotowitz, M., 1980, ppxxv).

Eiade refers to 'specialized initiations, which certain individuals undergo in order to transcend their human condition and become protégés of the Supernatural Beings or even their equals' (Eliade, M., 2003, pp.128-129). Jonah's resuscitation by Elijah can be seen as an instance of this. It also marked the child as being different in some way, which has also often been a characteristic of those destined to become shamans.

> A member of a community can become a medicine man or a shaman not only in consequence of a personal decision to acquire religious powers (the process called "the quest") but also through vocation ("the call"), that is, because he is forced by Superhuman Beings to become a medicine man or shaman (Eliade, M., 2003, pp.2-3).

In a similar manner, Jonah was forced by a Superhuman Being (God) to become a prophet.

When Jonah was first called on by God to act as a prophet, his reluctance to comply was typical of the way that prospective shamans would react to the 'call', knowing only too well what was likely to be in store for them. Eliade explains how just 'like any other religious vocation, the shamanic vocation is manifested by a crisis, a temporary derangement of the future shaman's spiritual equilibrium' (Eliade, M., 1964, p.xii). This is exactly what Jonah was destined to go through and helps to account for the way in which he initially tried to escape from the situation: 'Now the word of the Lord came

171

unto Jonah the son of Amittai, saying, Arise, go to Nineveh, that great city, and cry against it; for their wickedness is come up before me. But Jonah rose up to flee unto Tarshish from the presence of the Lord' (Jonah 1: 1-3).

The shamanic "gift" and the so-called "mastery" of spirits can be described as being double-edged: 'they are not actively sought but are rather imposed against the shaman's will, and as well as granting power also cause lifelong anguish. A similar view prevails in many shamanic cultures' (Vitebsky, P., 2001, p.57).

As Narby and Huxley point out, 'For men, the preparatory stage of shamanistic inspiration is in most cases very painful, and extends over a long time. The call comes in an abrupt and obscure manner, leaving the young novice in much uncertainty regarding it. He feels "bashful" and frightened; he doubts his own disposition and strength, as has been the case with all seers, from Moses down' (Narby, J., & Huxley, F., 2001, p.55). Jonah is unlikely to have been an exception and he was probably plagued with self-doubts too.

According to Scherman & Zlotowitz, Jonah was unwilling to follow his calling as he did not want to taste the bitterness of vilification that he had experienced when he had prophesied against Jerusalem, and he did not want to shame Israel by the comparison of its stubbornness with the obedience of Nineveh to the warning of God's prophet. However, all we know for sure from the Book of Jonah itself is that he was clearly reluctant and the reasons for this must consequently remain open to interpretation. (*op. cit.*, xxvi-xxviii)

What is clear, however, as Vitebsky shows, is that Jonah was not alone in finding it difficult to accept what fate had in store for him.

In Siberia, Mongolia and many other areas, people dread being called by the spirits to become shamans and resist for as long as they have the strength. Recently, in a remote area of Siberia, the local shaman died as an old man. He had tried

172

to pass on his secrets to his grandson but the grandson had repeatedly declined the gift, and later explained that he could not face the personal sacrifice which would be required of him, since a shaman's power is fed from the soul-force of his immediate family. His wife and children must therefore suffer poor health and early death as the shaman unintentionally sucks the life out of those with whom he lives (Vitebsky, P., 2001, p.22).

The storm that ensued was sent by God to punish Jonah but he saw no reason why the innocent sailors should suffer for his sins: 'And he said unto them, Take me up, and cast me forth into the sea; so shall the sea be calm unto you: for I know that for my sake this great tempest is upon you' (Jonah 1: 12). 'So they took up Jonah, and cast him forth into the raging sea: and the sea ceased her raging' (Jonah 1: 15).

It is at this point in the story that Jonah's initiation takes place: 'Now the Lord had prepared a great fish to swallow up Jonah. And Jonah was in the belly of the fish three days and three nights' (Jonah 1: 17). The parallels between this and the initiatory ordeal of the shaman are plain to see. 'The majority of initiatory ordeals more or less clearly imply a ritual death followed by resurrection or a new birth' (Eliade, M., 1958, p. xii). 'Initiatory death is indispensable for the beginning of spiritual life. Its function may be understood in relation to what it prepares: birth to a higher mode of being' (*Ibid.* p. xiv).
Jonah's own description of his experience, if we did not know where it comes from, could easily be mistaken for the description of a shamanic descent to the underworld: 'The waters compassed me about, even to the soul: the depth closed me round about, the weeds wrapped about my head. I went down to the bottoms of the mountains; the earth with her bars was about me for ever …' (Jonah 2: 5-6). As Eliade explains, 'He who has been successful in such an exploit no longer fears death; he has conquered a kind of bodily immortality, the goal of all heroic initiations' (Eliade, 1958, p.64).

Conducting the spiritual seeker into a new mode of being, one that involves a novel way of relating to existence, can be regarded as the main purpose of any initiatory experience. 'Whereas previously the seeker may have had only intimations of a different, hidden order of existence, through initiation he or she is granted a vision or a palpable sense of that "alternative" reality' (Feurstein, G., 1991, p.146). Jonah's experience of being swallowed by the whale enables him to pass beyond the profane, unsanctified condition of his former mode of existence, to put him in touch with the numinous dimension of existence known as spirit.

When a person is at a point of transition, the state of being 'in-between' states, the predicament Jonah found himself in, is known as liminality. 'Arnold van Gennep recognised long ago that these are moments when people switch from one social group and that they are times when loss of clear social definition invites danger: Consequently to control the danger they are subjected to ritual, what van Gennep called **rites of passage**' (Stone, A., 2003, p.63) and this is what God subjected Jonah to when he had him swallowed by the whale.

> The dreamer, thirsting for the shining heights, had first to descend into the dark depths, and this proves to be the indispensable condition for climbing any higher. The prudent man avoids the dangers lurking in these depths, but he also throws away the good which a bold but imprudent venture might bring (Jung, C.G., 1959, p.19).

This quote neatly summarizes the experience Jonah had to go through.

Then 'the word of the Lord came unto Jonah the second time, saying, Arise, go unto Nineveh, that great city, and preach unto it the preaching that I bid thee' (Jonah 3: 1-2). And this time Jonah did what he was told.

Although the parallels between the shaman and Jonah soon become apparent once we start to delve into his biography, what about Jonah as a storyteller? The answer is very simple. If Jonah had not been an effective storyteller, the people in Nineveh would never have believed his prophecies and would have had no reason to turn from their evil ways. Like Moses, he must surely have been a master of his craft.

Both the shaman and the prophet provide a stark contrast to the figure of the traditional priest. 'The priest usually differs from the medicine-man – and also from the prophet – precisely in the ecstasy, the being filled with the god, being in him as it were frozen or crystallized, the occasional miracle incorporated in ordered official actions and the cries of ecstatic possession in the monotonous intonation of the liturgy' (Van Der Leeuw, G., 1938, p.219).

Although it is not written in the Book of Jonah itself, according to Pinrkei d'Rabbi Eliezer (ch. 10) Jonah delivered another major prophecy in his lifetime, prior to his prophecy to the people of Nineveh – to the Jewish people. 'He was sent to warn the inhabitants of Jerusalem that the Holy City would be destroyed because of their sins. The people repented and, following the rule that an evil prophecy can be annulled by repentance, the city was saved' (Scherman, N. & Zlotowitz, M., 1980 Second Edition, p.xxvi).It is interesting to note that each time that they enjoyed a period of comparative peace and economic prosperity, the people of Israel turned from Yahweh and to the false gods of their neighbours.

> Only historical catastrophes [or the threat of such occurrences] brought them back to the right road by forcing them to look toward the true God. ... This return to the true God in the hour of disaster reminds us of the desperate gesture of the primitive, who, to rediscover the existence of the Supreme Being, requires the extreme of peril and the failure of all addresses to other divine forms [gods, ancestors, demons]. (Eliade, M., 1965, p.103).

We learn from Eliade that 'Ecstatic election is usually followed by a period of instruction, during which the neophyte is duly initiated by an old shaman. At this time the future shaman is supposed to master his mystical techniques and to learn the religious and mythological traditions of his tribe' (Eliade, M., 1964, p.110). Similarly, Jonah is then given a period of instruction by God. God teaches him how to show compassion and forgiveness through his own example – by creating, then destroying, a gourd to protect Jonah from the sun, which Jonah feels sorry for. And the book concludes with God asking the question: 'And should not I spare Nineveh, that great city, wherein are more than sixscore thousand persons that cannot discern between their right hand and their left hand; and also much cattle?' (Jonah 4: 11). Just like Carlos Castaneda in the Don Juan novels, Jonah has to learn from his mistakes.

> Initiatory sicknesses may be experienced as 'torture at the hands of demons or spirits, who play the role of masters of initiation, … ritual death [which is] experienced by the patient as a descent to Hell or an ascent to Heaven, … [and] resurrection to a new mode of being – the mode of "consecrated man," that is, a man who can personally communicate with gods, demons, and spirits (Eliade, M., 2003, p.91).

In Jonah's case, he can be said to have experienced ritual death when he was swallowed by the whale, and this was followed by his resurrection to a new mode of being, in which he was to serve as God's prophet.

'The purpose of the **descent** as universally exemplified in the myth of the hero is to show that only in the region of danger (watery abyss, cavern, forest, island, castle, etc.) can one find the "treasure hard to attain" (jewel, virgin, life-potion, victory over death). The dread and resistance which every natural human being experiences when it comes to delving too deeply into himself is, at bottom, the fear of the journey to Hades' (Jung, C.G., 1968 2nd Edition, pp.335-336). It can be seen, with the help of God or as the result of the circumstances that resulted from the storm, Jonah overcame his resistance and so found that victory over death.

According to Joseph Campbell, the imagery of schizophrenic fantasy perfectly matches that of the mythological hero journey, which he sees as consisting of a three-stage process: 1) separation, 2) initiation, and 3) return. 'A hero ventures forth from the world of common day into a region of supernatural wonder: fabulous forces are there encountered and a decisive victory is won: the hero comes back from this mysterious adventure with the power to bestow boons on his fellow men' (Campbell, J., 1973, pp.202-203). Whether Jonah ever actually existed or whether he ever underwent the experiences described the bible, we can never know for sure. However, there can be no doubt that the story of his journey clearly includes the three stages described by Campbell, which helps to account for the way it has withstood the test of time and still has a message for us today.

'Initiations, though following different paths, pursue the same end – to make the novice die to the human condition and to resuscitate him to a new, a trans-human existence' (Eliade, M., 1958, p.87). The path for Jacob was through the vision he had in his dream and the path for Jonah was through his ritual death when he was thrown overboard during the storm. For people today the path might be through a mid-life crisis – something like the 'male menopause' could even bring it on!

Journeying, Storytelling and Spiritual Intelligence

Before dealing with what has been called the third form of intelligence, it might be helpful to say a few words about the other two forms – IQ and EQ. IQ Tests were developed by Binet early in the 20th century and were frequently used to assess the potential of children in schools until quite recently. Tests of this type, however, have now fallen into disrepute. All they test is linguistic and logical-mathematical intelligence and this traditional definition of intelligence is now regarded as too narrow. We now know that 75% of teachers are sequential, analytical presenters but 70% of students do not actually learn this way! The educational psychologist most responsible for this change of attitude is Howard Gardner, the creator of the **Multiple Intelligence Theory**.

Gardner's work at the Boston University School of Medicine led to the identification of eight criteria for the existence of intelligence types: potential isolation by brain damage; the existence of prodigies such as autistic *savants*; an identifiable set of core operations; a distinctive developmental history along with a definable set of expert end-state performances; an evolutionary history; support from experimental psychological tasks; support from psychometric findings; and susceptibility to an encoding symbol system. These criteria are explained in detail in Gardner's *Frames of Mind* (1983).

Gardner originally identified seven intelligence types which satisfy the above criteria and our intelligence profiles consist of combinations of the different types: linguistic; logical-mathematical; spatial; bodily-kinesthetic; musical; interpersonal - the way we relate to others; and intrapersonal - our ability to self-evaluate. **Emotional Intelligence**, the term popularised by Daniel Goleman (1996) covers what Gardner refers to as interpersonal plus intrapersonal.

178

Gardner refers to Intelligences as potentials that will or will not be activated, depending upon the values of a particular culture, the opportunities available in that culture, and the personal decisions made by individuals and/or their families, schoolteachers, and others.

A student who believes that intelligence can be developed is likely to be persistent and adventurous. However, a learner who thinks that ability is fixed, is more likely to get upset when faced with failure as it can only be construed as evidence of inadequate ability. The fluid 'theory' of intelligence advocated by Gardner encourages students to stretch themselves.

In his book *Intelligence Reframed* Gardner adds to the original 'Magnificent Seven' **Naturalist Intelligence**, our talent for classifying and categorising. He also speculates on the possibility of there being both a spiritual intelligence and an existential intelligence but comes to no definite conclusions. Danah Zohar makes out a convincing case for their being a ninth kind, **Spiritual Intelligence** (Zohar, 2000). This will be the subject of the final part of this book.

Does the fact that we each have a unique profile mean that individual should be planned for each learner? Clearly this would be impractical and the solution lies in including material designed to appeal to each of the types in every lesson given. The table presented below lists classroom activities that cater for the different Intelligence types. However, this classification is clearly subjective and dependent on individual teaching styles. Moreover, it should also be pointed out that a number of the activities cater for more than one Intelligence type and could consequently be placed in more than one category:

179

ACTIVITIES TO DEVELOP THE INTELLIGENCES

*Linguistic Intelligence: group discussions / reading / completing worksheets / wordbuilding games / giving presentations / listening to lectures

*Logical-mathematical Intelligence: logic puzzles / problem solving / logical-sequential presentations / guided discovery

*Visual/Spatial Intelligence: charts / diagrams / mind maps / peripherals / storyboards / videos

*Bodily-kinesthetic Intelligence: Circle Dancing / Relaxation Exercises / Brain Gym / Craftwork

*Musical Intelligence: Songs / Background Music / Jazz Chants

*Interpersonal Intelligence: Circle Time / groupwork / pairwork / brainstorming / peer teaching / questionnaires

*Intrapersonal Intelligence: project work / self-study / learner diaries / personal goal setting / Pole-bridging activities / reflective learning activities

*Naturalist Intelligence: classifying & categorising activities / Background Music - in the form of sounds created in the natural world

*Spiritual Intelligence: guided visualisation / storytelling

It is important to differentiate between the **Learning Styles** referred to in Neuro-Linguistic Programming, and **Intelligence Types**. Gardner suggests that it is the decision about how to use one's favoured intelligences that reflects one's preferred style.

It is clear that unless teaching is multi-modal and caters for all the intelligence types, it will fail to reach all the learners in the group whichever approach to teaching is adopted. Another reason for teaching multi-modally is that with high levels of stimulus and challenge there are higher ratios of synapses (connections) to the neurons in the brain. This means more routes for higher order cognitive functioning. The optimal conditions for synaptic growth would include multiple complex connective challenges where, in learning, we are actively engaged in multi-sensory immersion experiences.

MI theory, according to Gardner, is an endorsement of three key propositions:

1. We are not all the same.
2. We do not all have the same kinds of minds.
3. Education works most effectively if these differences are taken into account rather than denied or ignored.

He suggests that the challenge of the next millennium is whether we can make these differences central to teaching and learning or whether we will instead continue to treat everyone in a uniform way. Gardner proposes "individually configured education" – an education that takes individual differences seriously, and crafts practices that serve different kinds of minds equally well.

> **Teaching is only demonstrating that it is possible. Learning is making it possible for yourself.**
> PAUL COELHO, *The Pilgrimage*

According to Danah Zohar, SQ (Spiritual Intelligence) is what we use to develop our longing and capacity for meaning, vision and value. It facilitates a dialogue between reason and emotion, between mind and body. SQ allows us to integrate the intrapersonal and the interpersonal, to transcend the gap between self and other. (*op. cit.*)

There is believed to be a built-in spiritual centre located among neural connections in the temporal lobes of the brain. On scans taken with positron emission topography these neural areas light up whenever research subjects are exposed to discussion of spiritual or religious topics. Neurobiologists have now dubbed the area of the temporal lobes concerned with religious or spiritual experience the 'God spot' or the 'God module'.

The brain's unitive experience emanates from synchronous 40 Hz neural oscillations that travel across the whole brain. According to Zohar, the 40 Hz oscillations are the neural basis of SQ, a third intelligence that places our actions and experience in a larger context of meaning and value, thus rendering them more effective. Everything possesses a degree of proto-consciousness but only certain special structures, like brains, have what is needed to generate full-blown consciousness. In this case, we conscious human beings have our roots at the origin of the universe itself. Our spiritual intelligence grounds us in the wider cosmos, and life has purpose and meaning within the larger context of cosmic evolutionary processes.

The indications of a highly developed SQ include:
the capacity to be flexible
a high degree of self- awareness
a capacity to face and use suffering
a capacity to face and transcend pain
the quality of being inspired by vision and values
a reluctance to cause unnecessary harm
a tendency to see the connections between diverse things
a marked tendency to ask 'Why?' or 'What if?' questions and to seek 'fundamental' answers
being 'field-independent' – possessing a facility for working against convention.

Peggy Ann Wright at Lesley College in Cambridge, Massachusetts, has studied a link between heightened temporal lobe activity and shamanistic experiences. These are soul journeys to distant realms of experience in order to communicate with spirits of the living and the dead, and to bring back healing advice. Wright's work has also shown that rhythmic drumming of the sort used in a vast range of spiritual rituals excites the temporal lobes and associated areas of the limbic system. (in Zohar, 2000).

Guided visualisation can also be used to excite the temporal lobes and the process can be used in the classroom. In a similar way, every time you introduce a tale starting *'once upon a time'*, you are inviting your audience to transcend their linear concepts of time and space and so enter a light state of trance. Consequently, both guided imagery and story telling can be used to facilitate the development of SQ.

For example, here is an American Indian story which deals with the subject of equality: it is used by some practitioners to develop SQ. Its purpose is to show that some people are so full of self-importance that they set themselves above the rest of us, who are however, equally to blame because we are prepared to bow down to them and to worship them as if they were gods. The American Indians believe humour is sacred and it is through the use of humour as a teaching tool that this story gets its message across:

THE DOGS HOLD AN ELECTION

Once a long time ago, the dogs were trying to elect a president. So one of them got up in the big dog convention and said: "I nominate the bulldog for president. He's strong. He can fight."
"But he can't run," said another dog. "What good is a fighter who can't run? He won't catch anybody."
Then another dog got up and said: "I nominate the greyhound, because he can definitely run.

183

But the other dogs objected: "He can run all right but he can't fight. When he catches up with somebody, what happens then? He gets beaten up, that's what! So all he's good for is running away.

Then an ugly little mongrel jumped up and said: "I nominate that dog for president who smells good underneath his tail."

And immediately an equally ugly mongrel jumped up and yelled: "I second the motion." At once all the dogs started sniffing underneath each other's tails. A big chorus went up: "Phew, he doesn't smell good under his tail."

"No, neither does this one."

"He's certainly no presidential prospect!"

"No, he's no good, either."

"This one certainly isn't the people's choice."

You may have noticed that the dogs are still sniffing underneath each other's tails. They're still looking for a good leader, and they still haven't found him.

The companions admitted to the high order of King Arthur's **Round Table** were bound to a recognition of their equality of companionship: they were bound by oath to assist each other at the hazard of their own lives, to attempt singly the most perilous adventures, to lead, when necessary, a life of monastic solitude, to fly to arms at the first summons, and never to retire from battle till they had defeated the enemy, unless night intervened and separated the combatants. What is reputed to be the top of the original table can now be seen in Winchester Cathedral.

The guide who helped you through the seventh chapter is now ready to show you how to **take your rightful place** at the Round Table.

Take a few deep breaths to help you relax. Breathe in the light and breathe out all your tightness. Feel the tension disappear stage by stage from the top of your head to the tips of your toes. Let your surroundings fade away as you gradually sink backwards through

184

time and actuality and pass through the gateway of reality into the dreamtime.

Sometimes, like all of us, you probably consider yourself unworthy and can't resist the temptation to compare yourself to others. And perhaps, like me, you went to a school where everyone was given a class position at the end of term and you always came near the bottom. Not to worry because help is close at hand, probably closer than you realize.

You enter the doorway of what appears to be a Cathedral. Your name is being called and you hear a fanfare of trumpets. As if in a dream, you are led down the central aisle. Smell the incense being burned and listen to the singing of the choir. Each of the stained glass windows in the walls depicts a scene from history – pictures of all the great artists, writers, composers, scientists, politicians, inventors and discoverers.

At the far end you see an enormous round table. All the seats are taken except for one. You look around at the faces and see all the people you've ever admired seated in a circle. Who should be sitting in the empty chair? Perhaps the teacher who used to read out the list of class positions at the end of each term, or the pupil who was always captain of the school team and who never picked you? Wait a minute? The people at the table seems to be pointing in your direction. You look behind you to see who might be there. After all, it can't possibly be you. You're not worthy to be anything more than just an observer. But when you turn around, there's nobody there. You look back at the Round Table, and this time the people there are even calling you by your name. Yes. There's no doubt about it. The final place has been reserved for you. You sit down and join the circle, too stunned to say anything.

You're probably wondering what you are doing here. We all do on our first occasion. You see, we were just like you once, no different. All of us, like you, doubted our worthiness but hid it from the rest of the world. Take a minute of clock time, equal to all the time you need, to ask yourself why the table is round, then the veil that's obscuring the truth will be lifted and everything will become clear to you.

We hope that by now you have found the answer. The truth is that all of us are equal, which is why nobody sits at the head. We all have different strengths and weaknesses and we are all unique. Nobody is better or worse, just different. But all of us share one thing in common. Like you we are part of the Great Mystery, the Oneness that gave birth to us. The time has come for you to claim your rightful place too, the place that is your birthright. So take a minute of clock time, equal to all the time you need, to reconnect with that force .....

If ever you should be plagued by self-doubts again, remember this scene. If ever you should feel isolated, then return to this Table. This chair is always yours. Now link hands with everyone present, to complete the circuit between us and to let the current flow. Take a minute of clock time, equal to all the time you need, to appreciate this special moment.

Now the time has come to return, back to the everyday world waiting for you on the other side. But you return with the recognition of your true worth and this will be with you forever. Never again will you have any cause to doubt your value. So retrace your steps now, back down the aisle, back past the stained glass windows, back, back, through time and actuality, back through the gateway between the two worlds, and back to the place you started from.

Take a deep breath, release it, open your eyes and stretch your arms and legs. Stamp your feet on the ground to make sure you're really back. Welcome home!

Here are two stories with the same theme of companionship and equality, one old and one modern.

PARTS OF THE BODY

One day all the Limbs of the Body, the Arms and Legs, got together and complained to the Stomach: "We're sick and tired of doing all the work while you just eat everything we collect without paying for it and we've decided to go on strike." So the Feet refused to walk, the Hands stopped holding things, the Eyes avoided seeing, the Ears became deaf, the Nose stopped smelling and the Tongue refused to taste.

The Stomach was most upset because he couldn't get food from anywhere and didn't know what to do. Sometimes the best thing in such situations is to do nothing and that's exactly what the Stomach did. He just lay down patiently and waited.

He didn't have to wait very long because the Arms and the Legs quickly lost all their strength. The Hands began to shake and the Feet began to tremble. The Eyes began to cry, the Ears started to ring like bells, the Nose began to run and the Tongue was as dry as a bone.

When the Stomach saw they had suffered enough, he began to speak: "Now you can see how foolish you've been. I digested the food you gave me to produce the energy you need to function."

When the Limbs heard these words, they felt very ashamed of their actions. "You're right. We've been very stupid. We need you as much as you need us and we'll never make the mistake of complaining again. We promise. You can be sure we've learnt our lesson!"

The following is a contemporary tale with the same theme:

IN THE GREENHOUSE

Gilbert Greensleeves was very proud of his tomato collection and his succulent, perfectly formed specimens regularly won him prizes in horticultural competitions all over the land. He tended his plants as if they were his babies and, in a way, they were as Gilbert and his wife had never been blessed with any children of their own. So he was most upset when he woke up one fine summer morning to find a terrible commotion going on in the greenhouse.

187

He rushed outside, still in his pyjamas, to see what the problem was and he found all the tomatoes having a heated argument. In fact, the dispute had got so out of hand that the tomatoes were almost coming to blows. He tried to calm them all down and to make them see sense but without success and was at a total loss as to what to do.

Fortunately, he knew a bit about relaxation techniques, which he'd learnt to help him cope with his pre-competition nerves, and in desperation he decided to try them out on his beauties. After all, he didn't want them to get themselves into a state, especially just before the annual finals. It wasn't easy but he eventually managed to attract their attention and to persuade them all to follow his instructions.

"Good. Now I'd like you make yourselves comfortable and close your eyes," he began. "Feel the tension gradually fade away from the tops of your juicy heads to the tips of your little green toes." Here he paused for a moment to give his words a chance to take effect and to produce the desired results. "Now focus on your heads," he continued "and become aware of the fibre that extends from your crown *chakra* and what it's connected to."

After a couple of minutes, one of the more forthcoming tomatoes, generally regarded as the leader of the pack, broke the silence. "But we're all connected to each other and we all come from the same source," he observed.

"That's it exactly," Gilbert Greensleeves replied. "So now you've solved one of the mysteries of life. When you fight against each other, you're only fighting against yourselves. And perhaps now you can be more understanding and tolerant towards one another in future." A hush descended over the greenhouse as all the tomatoes bowed their heads in shame. It was clear that they had all learnt their lesson and Gilbert returned to the house with his head held high, his mission having been accomplished.

And from that moment onwards, Gilbert Greensleeves never had another problem. His tomatoes lived in perfect harmony and won him even more prizes than before!

As Danah Zohar points out, it is important to emphasise that a mere sense of the spiritual does not guarantee that we can use it creatively in our lives. To have high SQ is to be able to use the spiritual to bring greater context and meaning to living a richer and more meaningful life, to achieve a sense of personal wholeness, purpose and direction.(*op.cit.*) Her work points the way to the use of both journeying and storytelling for the development of Spiritual Intelligence.

As we have already seen, Cahill and Halpern suggest that there are three distinct stages in ceremony which need to be honored for the experience to touch us deeply: Severance-leaving behind the everyday world, entering Sacred Time & Space – going beyond ourselves, and Reincorporation – returning with new self-knowledge. (Cahill and Halpern,1991)

Einstein famously remarked that we cannot solve problems from within the mind frame that created the problems in the first place. Any time that we step outside our assumptions or habitual way of seeing things by entering Sacred Time & Space, we are experiencing what Danah Zohar calls our SQ (Spiritual Intelligence) and to some small extent, at least, using it for the purpose of self-development.

Reincorporation, like recollection, entails the bringing together of our world inside and our world outside, the meeting of the deep, inner self and its innate wisdom or spiritual intelligence with the outer ego and its worldly concerns, strategies and activities. Recollection can be defined as SQ in action.

In a story telling session, you leave the everyday world behind you the moment the storyteller says '*once upon a time*', you're transported beyond yourself into another setting during the telling of the tale, and you return with new self-knowledge if the story worked as a metaphor for you.

Through guided imagery, one can leave behind the stress of daily life through relaxation, and go beyond oneself

The Shaman and the Storyteller

by entering a light state of trance, returning with the visions gained on the journey.

When you are in power and in control of your life, there is nothing you are unable to do. Ma Liang, in the Chinese folktale that follows, even has power over the Elements. You too can have a magic brush like the boy in the story - all you need is belief in yourself:

THE BOY WITH THE MAGIC BRUSH

Once upon a time in a little village, a poor boy named Ma Liang was born. It was not long before his parents died, so he became an orphan. To survive he had to work for a landlord. He worked day and night.

One day, after finishing his work, he returned to his shabby bed in his shabby little house. When he passed the window of the landlord's house, he saw an artist drawing a picture for the landlord. What a beautiful scene it was! Ma Liang admired it very much. He wanted so much to have a brush to draw with.

"Would you give me a brush to draw?" he asked the landlord.

"You? Ha!" replied the landlord. "A beggar wanting to draw! Are you joking?"

At this, everyone present laughed at Ma Liang. This made him so angry that he made up his mind there and then to learn how to draw. And he vowed to draw only for the poor.

From there on, he began to practise drawing. Whatever he saw and wherever he was, he drew. Because he had no brush, he used a branch or whatever else he could get his hands on. He had no paper, so he often drew in the sand.

Years went by and Ma Liang became a good artist. Everything he drew was as lovely as if it were real. He only wished he had a brush!

One night, after practising drawing, he went to bed. Because he was so tired he began to dream very quickly. Suddenly he was in a different place. A brook led off into the distance with all kinds of flowers on both banks, and an old man stood in front of him. Ma Liang was too surprised to say a word!

"You want your own brush, don't you?" the old man asked.

"Yes, I do!" replied Ma Liang.

"Well then, I will give you a brush, but remember that you promised to draw only for the poor." With this, the old man disappeared.

"But where is the brush?" Ma Liang wondered anxiously. "Where?"

When Ma Liang awoke, he realised that it had only been a dream, but to his surprise there was a real brush in his bed. He was very pleased. The first thing he did was to draw a cock on the wall. No sooner had he finished the drawing than the cock stepped out of the wall and came to life. Ma Liang had received a magic brush!

Ma Liang began to draw for the poor. Because he could draw whatever he wanted and whatever he drew came to life, he did a lot of good with his brush. It was not long before the emperor heard the news and ordered his soldiers to bring Ma Liang to him.

The emperor met Ma Liang in his big hall. The emperor said. "I have heard that you have a magic brush that can bring whatever you draw to life. Is this true?

"Yes," replied Ma Liang.

"Then give it to me," ordered the emperor.

"No, it's mine," responded Ma Liang.

"How dare you say that?" fumed the emperor. "I am the emperor. You must obey me!" At this, two guards snatched the brush from Ma Liang's hands.

The emperor put the brush into the hands of the most respected painter in the kingdom and asked him to draw something, but his painting did not become real. Seeing that his plan was not working, the emperor tried to persuade Ma Liang to draw something. Ma Liang, however, decided to teach the emperor a lesson.

"What would you like me to draw for you?" asked Ma Liang.

"Gold. A hill made of gold," replied the emperor.

191

Ma Liang began to draw, not a hill of gold, but a picture of the ocean.

"Fool, I want gold!" roared the emperor.

So Ma Liang drew an island of gold in the ocean.

"Now draw a ship," ordered the emperor. A ship soon appeared in the picture. The emperor hurriedly jumped into the ship with his guards and prime minister to set sail for the isalnd of gold. The ship sat quietly, so the emperor once again ordered Ma Liang to draw, this time wind so that the ship could move.

Ma Liang wasted no time in drawing a violent wind that almost capsized the ship. The emperor screamed for Ma Liang to stop, but Ma Liang only drew more and more bad weather until the ship disappeared out of sight.

Ma Liang continued drawing for the poor. Both he and the poor were happy.

In the story of Noah's Ark the water of the flood serves as a means of selection – deciding who deserves to live and who deserves to die. In the story of the bird and her chicks, the bird takes on the role of the Creator to make that decision. It's a traditional Yiddish tale which takes a humorous look at the difficult problem that many of us will have to face one day:

A FABLE OF A BIRD AND HER CHICKS

Once upon a time a mother bird who had three chicks wanted to cross a river. So she put the first one under her wing and started flying across. As she flew she said, "Tell me, child, when I'm old and frail, will you carry me under your wing as I'm carrying you now?"

"Of course," replied the chick. "What a question!"

"Ah," said the mother bird, "you're lying." With that she let the chick slip, and it fell into the river and drowned.

The mother went back for the second chick, which she took under her wing. Once more as she was flying across the river, she said, "Tell me, child, when I'm old and frail, will you carry me under your wing the way I'm carrying you now?"

"Of course," replied the chick. "What a question!"

"Ah," said the mother bird, "you're lying." With that she let the second chick slip, and it also drowned.

Then the mother went back for the third chick, which she took under her wing. Once more she asked in mid-flight, "Tell me, child, when I'm old and frail, will you carry me under your wing the way I'm carrying you now?"

"No, mother," replied the third chick. "How could I? By then I'll have chicks of my own to carry."

"Ah, my dearest child," said the mother bird, "you're the one who tells the truth." And with that she carried the third chick to the other bank of the river.

A number of factors contribute to the way in which an individual approaches learning experiences including environmental, emotional, sociological, physical and psychological. It is emotion, not logic, that drives our attention, meaning-making and memory. This suggests the importance of eliciting curiosity, suspense, humour, excitement, joy and laughter. Story telling can provide an ideal means of achieving this:

THE LEARNING PLACE

This is the story of Alessandra, a young woman who leaves her parents' home to make her own way in the world. She's looking for something more than the familiar everyday routine of her family, the challenge of the new and unfamiliar. So she travels to the Learning Place, a special place visited by seekers of all kinds, in the land known as Dan Glen. She arrives in Autumn, just as the leaves are beginning to change to colours of deep red, orange and yellow, and the trees themselves are turning within for the winter.

Alessandra's feeling a bit nervous because she's never been to Dan Glen before and doesn't understand the language spoken there. So when she arrives and hears the people speaking so quickly, she gets frightened and thinks perhaps she's made a big mistake. Many learners are based in the Centre besides herself and she notices they don't appear to be afraid. In fact, they seem to be enjoying life to the full and this helps to reassure her

Alessandra walks around the Centre feeling rather lost until she meets one of the welcome guides who helps new arrivals to feel at home. The guide's name is Karelov. Karelov is a kind, gentle man who soon makes her feel comfortable listening to his native language. She's surprised at how relaxed and confident she feels with her guide. Her understanding of the new language grows quickly, and before long she's beginning to use the language too. Karelov recognizes that Alessandra has all the abilities she needs to do very well.

With Karelov's support and encouragement, Alessandra begins to open her mind and heart to all the new opportunities around her. Karelov spends many hours with Alessandra and the other new arrivals. He tells them lots of stories, he plays lots of games and listens with patience and interest. They all learn quickly without even realizing it's happening and Alessandra's confidence quickly grows. She makes friends with the other new arrivals in her group and she recognizes that their situations are similar to her own.

One of these friends, Eduardo, invites her to the annual festival of dance in Dan Glen. Karelov has taught them the traditional dances and they demonstrate their skills at the festival with ease and delight. Even the natives are impressed and congratulate them on the naturalness and ease of their performance.

During one of the breaks, a traditional dance instructor called Killjoy asks them how many hours and days they must have struggled to reach such a high standard. He can't believe it when they tell him that it was no struggle at all and that they enjoyed every minute of it. He thinks they must be lying. Alessandra and Eduardo become a little confused and wonder if they did something wrong. They can't understand all this analysis of their learning which just happened so naturally.

At this moment Karelov and his partner Bella, who are also attending the dance, invite the young couple to join them in a dance for four. They tell Karelov about their conversation with the old dance instructor and Karelov smiles. He explains that unfortunately there are still teachers like Killjoy in the Centre with old-fashioned beliefs about how learning takes place. Killjoy, it seems, has forgotten that learning can be an enjoyable experience and that when people feel relaxed they can produce their best work. Alessandra and Eduardo realize from their own recent experiences that what Karelov is saying is true and a smile of recognition appears on the young couple's faces as they join Karelov and his partner for the dance.

The next day Karelov announces to Alessandra and the rest of the group that their initiation is now complete. They have all mastered naturally and with ease a basic understanding of the language and they are ready to move on. Their understanding of themselves and others has grown and so has their confidence. The friendships will last, the pleasant memories will remain, and the ending is just a beginning. As Karelov concludes his remarks, he invites everyone to hold hands and to join him in a circle, a circle of strength and unity.

Alessandra has since become a fine teacher herself and Eduardo is now working as an interpreter. And we leave them to continue their journey through life, following easily and naturally the best guide of all – the Karelov who resides within them.

Appendix One:
Story Openings and Endings

At the time when men and animals were all the same and spoke the same language ... (Traditional Navajo)

And that is how it is to this day.

Long, long ago, when some folk were already dead and others not yet born, there lived a ... (Tartar)

My story is done. But this story will go on, as long as grass grows and rivers run. (Native American)

Long ago in Estonia, when the people didn't have bathtubs...

This is what the Old Ones told me when I was a child... (Traditional Cherokee opening & ending)

In a certain kingdom, in a certain land, in a little village, there lived... (Russian)

But that is another story.

It all happened long ago, and believe it or not, it is all absolutely true. (Traditional Irish opening)

Well, whether it was false or true, the tale spread far and near, because the tale was fun to hear. (Saami)

Long, long ago, soon after sky and earth had become separated so that there was room for trees to grow and the tribes of men to move between them, many gods and spirits still lived in the world. (Maori)

And they lived happily ever after... or if they didn't, it's none of our business.

Many years ago, in a time when memory was young... (Indian)

That's the flourish (priskazka) just for fun; the real tale (skazka) has not yet begun... (Russian)

They feasted and they drank, and if the wine hadn't run out, I'd still be there with them instead of here talking to you.

A story, a story, let it come, let it go. (Traditional West African opening)

We shall exist as long as our stories are moist with our breath. (Navajo saying)

In the old, old, half-forgotten times, before the gardens of Tartary were overrun with weeds, there lived... (Tartar)

And the last person to tell that story - is standing here before you!

Once there was, one day there will be: this is the beginning of every fairy tale. There is no 'if' and no 'perhaps,' the three-legged stool unquestionably has three legs. (Breton)

In that town there was a well and in that well there was a bell. And that is all I have to tell. (Russian)

Once upon a time, and a very good time too, though it was not in my time, nor your time, nor for the matter of that in any one's time... (English Fairy Tales)

When the heart overflows, it comes out through the mouth. (Ethiopian)

There was, there was, and yet there was not (Georgian)

And ever since then, that is the way it has been.

This is my story which I have told you. If it be sweet, tell it to someone again and then some of the thanks will come back to me. (African)

And that's the end of that!

Once upon a time and a time before that... (Scandinavian)

And as far as anyone knows, they are living there still to this day.

Long before you and I were born, there lived... (Tartar)

It was not in my time, it was not in your time, but it was in somebody's time. (Irish)

And so it was, and so it is.

We do not really mean it. We do not really mean it, but they say... (Ashanti)

If you don't believe me, go see for yourself.

Long years ago, in the early ages of the world... (Hungarian)

They lived happily ever after and were never bothered again.

Far away in a hot country, where the forests are very thick and dark, and the rivers very swift and strong, there once lived... (African)

In olden times, in times when rams were still without horns and sheep without tails, there lived... (Kazakh)

Once there was and twice there wasn't...

Before the beginning of time, before the beginning of everything, before there was a beginning...

In a land that never was in a time that could never be...

In a place, neither near nor far, and a time, neither now nor then...

In the olden times when wishing still helped...

Long ago, so long ago, I wasn't there or I wouldn't be here now to tell you the tale...

Long ago when the earth was new... / Long, long ago when stones were soft...

Once upon a time what happened did happen - and if it had not happened, you would never have heard this story. (Andrew Lang)

Such things do happen, you know. (Russian gypsy)

Once upon a time, when the grass grew greener, the trees grew taller, and the sun shone more brightly than it does today, there was...

Once upon a time, so long ago, nobody but the storytellers remember...

I hope you won't fail to be pleased by my tale. For a pot full of butter, I'll tell you another. (Russian)

Appendix Two: The Art of Storytelling

Whenever people meet, stories are told as they have been since time immemorial. Storytelling is an oral tradition and because of the issues which have been worked through by the telling of the stories, story-telling has contributed to the creation of the great epics of the world. The storytellers themselves have been described as the bridge to other times and ancient teachings and the telling of the stories helps to keep these teachings alive. The children of future generations learn from the storytellers and apply lessons of the stories to their own lives.

The earliest stories were probably chants or songs of praise for the natural world in pagan times. Later, dance and music accompanied stories. The storyteller would become the entertainer for the community and the historian, musician and poet too. The oral tales that were passed on from one generation to the next by word of mouth included epics, myths, parables, fables, fairy and folk tales.

The art of storytelling was particularly popular from around AD400 to 1500. Storytellers would travel around visiting markets, villages, towns and royal courts. They gathered news, swapped stories and learned regional tales in the process. When popular tales began to be printed cheaply in pamphlets known as chap-books and sold by peddlers, their popularity started to wane. Unfortunately with the advent of the mass media, the storyteller has become more or less extinct. The telling of stories can encourage children to explore their unique expressiveness, and can heighten their ability to communicate thoughts and feelings in an articulate, lucid manner. These benefits transcend the art experience to support daily life skills. In our fast-paced, media-driven world, storytelling can be a nurturing way to remind children that their spoken words are powerful, that listening is important, and that clear communication between people is an art. Becoming verbally proficient can contribute to a person's ability to resolve interpersonal conflict non-violently. Negotiation, discussion, and tact are peacemaking skills. Being able to express one's thoughts and feelings is important for a child's safety. Clear communication is the first step to being able to ask for help when it is needed.

Both telling a story and listening to a well-told tale encourages the imagination. Developing the imagination can contribute to self-confidence and personal motivation as learners envision themselves competent and able to accomplish their hopes and dreams.

Storytelling based on traditional folktales is a gentle way to guide young people toward constructive personal values by presenting imaginative situations in which the outcome of both wise and unwise actions and decisions can be seen.

If you wish to play the role of storyteller, it is obviously important to know your story but this does not necessarily mean memorizing the words. You can do that if you want to, but the main thing is to know what happens to whom and when it is supposed to happen. One way of accomplishing this is to make an outline of the story to study. Another way is to imagine a picture for each part of the story with all the important things in the picture. Any special parts of the presentation such as poetry or complex phrases can be learned by heart and/or you can print them out on cue cards for reference. The more you repeat them out loud, the easier it will be to say them, whether you memorize them or not. For a first time situation it is a good idea to use stories you are confident with from previous occasions because the knowledge that you are well prepared helps diminish nervousness.

If possible, check out the space before the actual telling. If there is something that needs to be set up or changed, something to be planned, do it early, before you tell. Anticipate some of the things which might go wrong and know the strategies you will use to deal with any problems that might crop up. Make sure you have a fall-back position or some extra material up your sleeve to use if necessary. Remember that most of the things which are not right will probably only be noticed by you. Deal with everything you need to deal with beforehand, then forget about those things. When you get up to tell, it is time to concentrate on the listeners.

Keep the introduction and explanation as brief as possible. You may want to memorize some opening lines to make sure you leave nothing to chance and to show the audience that you know what you are doing; from then on it is up to them. As for the ending, take your time, but not the next speaker's. Be on, be good, and be off (vaudevillians' rule). Prepare a clean punch line or closing comment to finish with. "And that's the story of __," will do. And remember to thank your audience too.

Making mistakes is a natural part of performing. It is not a question of what to do if you make a mistake, but simply a matter of when you make a mistake. The most important thing is to stay calm and keep going. The audience does not know you have made a mistake unless you tell them so; do not draw attention to the problem by admitting to it or apologising. As far as they know, the way you told the story is the way you meant to tell it.

When you look out at the people listening to you, avoid anyone who makes you nervous. Try to find the people who make you feel safe. There is no reason to be scared of your audience. Your audience is (usually) your friend. They want you to succeed. And, since many of them are also nervous about talking in front of people, they will be sympathetic if things go wrong. Obviously, this sympathy is somewhat dependent on the venue and whether people pay to see you perform.

The nervousness you feel before going on is your performance energy. That is what will get you up on stage and into your story. And if you do not feel it, your performance will probably fall flat. The energy you feel is an instinctive reaction to stress. The body knows something is about to happen and is preparing for action. However, the emotional content is entirely conscious. Research shows that physiologically, fear, anger, excitement are all identical. The body is reacting in the same way. Your mind determines how you react to those stimuli and your emotions are under your control. With some practice, you can control whether it is fear or excitement running through your head before going on.

If you suffer badly from nerves, the Zen concept of No-Self as an approach to the problem can prove to be helpful – 'There is no teller... only the tale'. In this way you disappear for yourself as well as for the listeners. And if you have disappeared then there is no one to be nervous for.

An alternative approach is to make use of a Talking Stick (an American Indian tradition) which you pick up when you tell and hand to others when they tell. It helps to connect you to those legions over the centuries who have told stories and to remind you that you that you have an ancient responsibility to both audience and story. This carries you well beyond the awareness of nervousness. The nervousness is still there but now it is harnessed to bringing out the life in that story. The idea is to make your focus the responsibility to your audience and your story rather than focusing on yourself. Let go of yourself and think about the people you are telling the story to. Pay attention to them and you won't be thinking of yourself and you won't be nervous.

Guided visualisation can also be an effective tool. Sitting in some quiet place, imagine as clearly as possible that you are preparing to perform - employing all your senses - the sights, sounds, smells, and feelings associated with these pre-performance moments. Be as specific and detailed in your imaging as possible. When you have placed yourself as fully as possible into the pre-performance context, imagine yourself feeling completely confident--fearless. Imagine how great it would be to feel that way, rather than scared. Then continue on with the imagined performance: you present your material--solidly, and with confidence. Imagine the smoothness and grace with which you will make your presentation. Imagine your heart keeping a steady pace instead of racing. Imagine your breath deep and full, not shallow and shaky. In other words, paint an accurate and detailed mental image of every step of the process - the way you've experienced it so many times before – but with a successful outcome. Once you have experienced success in non-ordinary reality in this way, it becomes that much easier to achieve in this reality

Slowing down your breathing can help to control nervousness too. If you must focus on yourself, then focus on your breath. Breathing is the most important thing for life. If you are nervous, if you are scared, or feel any way you don't want to feel, then think about your breath and control it. Deep breaths - in through your nose - out through your mouth. Once you have your breath under control, you can do anything.

One way to practise storytelling with others is to pick a partner and sit facing each other, close enough to have your knees touching. Have other partners on either side of you so you are in two long lines all up close against each other, and all facing your respective partners. One person in each pair starts the story and after thirty seconds to a minute says, 'and', and then 'throws' the story to the person opposite to continue. That person makes up the next short segment, says 'and' and then passes the story back to the first person again. The story unfolds by being passed backwards and forwards this way between the same two partners.

BIBLIOGRAPHY

Allen, B. (2000) *Last of the Medicine Men*, London: BBC Worldwide Ltd.

Ahlback, T. (ed.) (1993) *The Problem of Ritual*, Stockholm, Sweden: Almqvist & Wiksell International.

Beckerlegge, G. (2001) *From Sacred Text to Internet*, Aldershot: Ashgate/Milton Keynes, The Open University.

Berman, M. (2000) *The Power of Metaphor*, Carmarthen: Crown House.

Berman, M., (2002 2nd Edition) *A Multiple Intelligences Road to an ELT Classroom*, Carmarthen: Crown House (first published 1998).

Blacker, C. (1999) *The Catalpa Bow A Study in Shamanic Practices in Japan*, Japan Library, *an imprint of Curzon Press Ltd.*

Cahill, S., & Halpern, J. (1991) *The Ceremonial Circle Shamanic Practice, Ritual and Renewal*, London: Mandala.

Campbell, J. (1973) *Myths to Live by*, London: Souvenir Press.

Chryssides, G. D. (1999) *Exploring New Religions*, London: Cassell.

Coelho, P. (1997) *The Pilgrimage*, London: Harper Collins.

Coelho, P. (2000) *By the River Piedra I Sat Down and Wept*, London: Harper Collins.

Doore, G. (Ed.) (1988) *Shaman's Path: Healing, Personal Growth and Empowerment*, Boston, Massachusetts: Shambhala Publications.

Drury, N., (1989) *The Elements of Shamanism*, Dorset: Element Books.

Edsman, C.M. (ed.) (1967) *Studies in Shamanism*, Stockholm: Almqvist & Wiksell.

Eliade, M. (1950) *Forgotten Religions* (ed V. Ferm), New York

Eliade, M. (1957) *The Sacred and the Profane: The Nature of Religion*, New York: Harper & Row.

Eliade, M. (1965) *The Myth of the Eternal Return*, Harper (originally published in 1949).

Eliade, M. (1969) The *Quest: History and Meaning in Religion.* London: University of Chicago Press.

Eliade, M. (1989) *Shamanism: Archaic techniques of ecstasy*, London: Arkana (first published in the USA by Pantheon Books 1964).

Eliade, M. (1991) *Images and Symbols,* New Jersey: Princeton University Press (The original edition is copyright Librairie Gallimard 1952).

Eliade, M. (2003) *Rites and Symbols of Initiation*, Putnam, Connecticut: Spring Publications (originally published by Harper Bros., New York, 1958).

207

Feurstein, G. (1991) *Holy Madness: the shock tactics and radical teachings of crazy-wise adepts, holy fools, and rascal gurus*, New York: Paragon House.

Gagan, Jeannette M. (1998) *Journeying: where shamanism and psychology meet*, Santa Fe, NM: Rio Chama Pubications.

Gardner, H. (1983) *Frames of Mind*, New York: Basic Books.

Gardner, H. (1993) *Multiple Intelligences – The Theory in Practice*, New York: Basic Books.

Gardner, H. (1999) *Intelligence Reframed*, New York: Basic Books.

Giddens, A. (1993) *Sociology*, Cambridge: Polity Press.

Goleman, D. (1996) *Emotional Intelligence*, UK: Bloomsbury.

Grinder & Bandler (1981) *Trance Formations*, Utah: Real People Press.

Halifax, J. (1987) 'Shamanism, Mind, and No Self' in Nicholson, S. (comp.) *Shamanism: An Extended View of Reality*, p.220, Wheaton: The Theosophical Publishing House.

Harner, M. (1990 Third Edition) *The Way of the Shaman*, Harper & Row (first published by Harper & Row in 1980).

Heelas, P. (1996) *The New Age Movement*, Oxford: Blackwell Publishers Ltd.

Herbert, D. (ed.) (2001) *Religion and Social Transformations*, Aldershot: Ashgate/Milton Keynes, The Open University.

Hoppal, Mihaly (1987) "Shamanism: An Archaic and/or Recent Belief System" in *Shamanism: An Extended View of Reality*, (comp. by Shirley Nicholson): The Theosophical Publishing House.

Horwitz, J. "Shamanic Rites seen from a Shamanic Perspective in Ahlback, T. (ed) 1993 *The Problem of Ritual*, Stockholm, Sweden: Almquist & Wiksell International.

Houston J. (1987a) *The Search for the Beloved*, Los Angeles: Tarcher.

Houston, J. (1987b) The Mind and Soul of the Shaman. In Shirley Nicholson (ed.) *Shamanism. An Extended View of Reality*, Wheaton: The Theosophical Publishing House, pp.vii-xiii).

Hultkrantz, A. (1979) *The Religions of the American Indians*, Berkeley: California.

Hunt, D.G. (1999) *Georgian Folk Tales*, Tbilisi, Georgia: Mirani Publishing House.

Ingermann, S. (1993) *Welcome Home: Following Your Soul's Journey Home*, New York: Harper Collins Publishers.

James, W. (1982) *The Varieties of Religious Experience*, Harmondsworth Middlesex: Penguin Books Ltd. (first published in the United States of America by Longmans, Green, and Co., 1902).

Jones, R.A. (1986) *Emile Durkheim: An Introduction to Four Major Works*. Beverly Hills, CA: Sage Publications, Inc.

Jung, C.G. (1959) *The Archetypes and the Collective Unconscious*, London: Routledge & Keegan Paul.

Jung, C.G. (1968 2nd Edition) *Psychology and Alchemy*, London: Routledge & Keegan Paul.

Jung, C.G. (1977) *The Symbolic Life*, London and Henley: Routledge & Keegan Paul.

Kirk, G.S. (1970) *Myth: Its Meaning and Function in Ancient and Other Cultures*, University of California Press, Berkeley and Los Angeles: University of California Press.

Kirsch, J. (1999) *Moses*, New York: Ballantine.

Kronberg, R., & Mckissack, P. (1990) *A Piece Of The Wind*, San Francisco: Harper.

Lewis, I.M. (2003 Third Edition) *Ecstatic Religion: a study of shamanism and spirit possession,* London: Routledge (first published 1971 by Penguin Books).

Maddox, J. L. (2003) *Shamans and Shamanism*, Dover Publications Inc. (originally published in 1923 by the Macmillan Company, New York, under the title *The Medicine Man: A Sociological Study of the Character and Evolution of Shamanism*).

Meadows, K. (1991) *Shamanic Experience. A Practical Guide to Contemporary Shamanism*, Shaftesbury: Element.

Mumm, S. (ed) (2002) *Religion Today: A Reader*, Aldershot: Ashgate/Milton Keynes, The Open University

Narby, J., & Huxley, F. (2001) *Shamans Through Time*, High Holborn, London: Thames & Hudson Ltd.

Nicholson, S. (ed.) (1987) *Shamanism. An Extended View of Reality*, Wheaton: The Theosophical Publishing House.

Otto, R. (1958) *The Idea of the Holy*, Oxford: Oxford University Press (first published by Oxford University Press, London 1923).

Pearson, J. (ed.) (2002) *Belief Beyond Boundaries: Wicca, Celtic Spirituality and the New Age*, Aldershot Ashgate/Milton Keynes, The Open University.

Radin, P. (1957) *Primitive Religion*, Dover Publications Inc. (first published in 1937 by the Viking Press.

Radin, P. (1983) *African Folktales*, New York: Schocken Books.

Rasmussen, K. (1921-24) *Intellectual Culture of the Caribou Eskimo*, Report of the Fifth Thule Expedition, vol. VII, No. 2.

Rennie, B. S. (1996) *Reconstructing Eliade: making sense of religion*, Albany: State University of New York Press.

Rutherford, W. (1986) *Shamanism: the foundations of magic*, Wellingborough Northamptonshire: The Aquarius Press.

Scherman, N., & Zlotowitz, M. (1980 Second Edition) *Yonah/Jonah*, Brooklyn, N.Y. Mesorah Publications Ltd.

Seligman, M.E.P. (1975), *Helplessness*, San Francisco: Freeman and Co.

Shirokogoroff, S. (1935) *Psychomental Complex of the Tungus*, London: Kegan Paul, Tranch Trubnor.

Smart, N. (1998 Second Edition) *The World's Religions*, Cambridge, Cambridge University Press (first published 1989).

Smith, A. (1996) *Accelerated Learning in the Classroom*, UK: Network Educational Press.

Smith, A. (1998) *Accelerated Learning in Practice*, UK: Network Educational Press.

Stone, A. (2003) *Explore Shamanism*, UK: Loughborough: Heart of Albion Press.

Trubshaw, B. (2003) *Explore Mythology*, Loughborough: Heart of Albion Press.

Van Der Leeuw, G. (1938) *Religion In Essence & Manifestation*, London: George Allen & Unwin Ltd., (The German original *Phanomenologie der Religion* published in Tubingen 1933).

Van Gennep, A. (1960) The Rites of Passage, Chicago: University of Chicago Press (original work published 1909).

Vitebsky, P. (2001) *The Shaman*, London: Duncan Baird (first published in Great Britain in 1995 by Macmillan Reference Books).

Walsh, R. N. (1990) *The Spirit of Shamanism*, London: Mandala.

Wolffe, J., (ed.) (2002) *Global Religious Movements in Regional Context*, Aldershot Ashgate/Milton Keynes, The Open University.

Zohar, H., & Marshall, I. (2000) *Spiritual Intelligence The Ultimate Intelligence*, London: Bloomsbury.

WEB ARTICLES AND WEBSITES

Berman, M., (2001) *ELT Through Multiple Intelligences*, www.netlearnpublications.com

Cox, A. an adaptation of "Bundles of Troubles, Bundles of Blessings" in the book - *A Piece Of The Wind*, by Ruthilde Kronberg and Patricia McKissack, Harper, San Francisco, 1990. It was found on Allison Cox's website: www.dancingleaves.com [accessed 28/07/04].

Durkheim, E., (1858-1917) see *"Durkheim Home Page"*: http://www.relst.uiuc.edu/durkheim/ [accessed 11/09/04].

Eagle's Wing Centre for Contemporary Shamanism. http://www.shamanism.co.uk/ [accessed 29/07/04].

Harner, M., *"Shamanism: Foundation for Shamanic Studies"* http://www.shamanism.org/ [accessed 29/07/04].

Horwitz, J & Høst, A. *Scandinavian Center for Shamanic Studies* [http://www.shaman-center.dk/ [accessed 29 July 2004]

Maley, A., article in the free E-zine, *HLT Magazine*: http://www.hltmag.co.uk/sept04/ [accessed 30/09/04].

Matthews, John and Caitlin, *" Hallowquest Newsletter"*: http://www.hallowquest.org.uk/ [accessed 29/07/04].

Paksoy, H.B., " *Central Asia's New Dastans*" (previously published in *Central Asian Survey* (Oxford) Vol. 6, No. 1,1987.Pp.75-92.):
http://www.euronet.nl/users/turkfed/mahmud.htm [accessed 10/09/04].

Sheppard,T.,"*...Storytelling-Resources...*"
http://www.timsheppard.co.uk/story/ [accessed 06/04/04].

Whitaker, D. *"The Oral Torah in the Hebrew Scriptures"*,
http: //www hope-of-israel.org/oraltorh.htm[accessed 20/07/04].